In Search of

RAMSDEN & CARR

In Search of
RAMSDEN
&CARR

Helen Ashton

UNICORN

First published by Unicorn
an imprint of the Unicorn Publishing Group LLP, 2018
101 Wardour Street
London W1F 0UG

www.unicornpublishing.org

10 9 8 7 6 5 4 3 2 1

ISBN 978-1-911604-15-0

Cover design Unicorn Publishing Group
Typeset by Vivian@Bookscribe

Printed and bound in Great Britain

CONTENTS

Dedication

⁎⁘⁘⁘⁘⁙⁙⁙⁘⁛⁚⁛

Dedicated to my grandchildren,
Peter, James, Katie, Carl, Mimi and Thea

INTRODUCTION

My first introduction to the name of Omar Ramsden came when I was researching the lives of my ancestors from Barbados, particularly my Great Aunt Alice Cumberbatch. As children, we had often heard of 'The Cumberbatch Trophy', commissioned by her in 1931. It was, and still is, presented to the person or company who made the greatest contribution to air safety in the preceding year. This is arranged through The Honourable Company of Air Pilots, formerly GAPAN, the Guild of Air Pilots and Navigators. When I began to research the trophy I found it was made by Omar Ramsden. A year or two later a cousin mentioned that Omar's son had married another cousin and that members of the family had various pieces made by him around their houses. Later I heard that this marriage had been annulled and that the son was a stepson. I was intrigued; at first it was just part of my family history, but as I slowly found out more and more about Ramsden and Alwyn Carr, his friend and colleague for many years, the more it became a story of its own, and so the search began in earnest.

When I first thought about gathering material on them, I wondered whether there would be enough information about their lives to make it worthwhile; it seemed that there was something of a mystique surrounding them. In 2002, on 9 August, for example, Ramsden had the honour of having his date of death noted under 'Anniversaries' in *The Times*. The same occurred in 2003, but it was the anniversary of his birth that was mentioned, though mistakenly given as 1878 rather than 1873. The mistake was repeated for the next two years.

There was also the need to investigate the context of a 1973 catalogue which was highly critical of Ramsden.[1] Produced by Birmingham City Museum and Art Gallery to accompany an exhibition on the 100th anniversary of his birth, the catalogue contained several factual errors in the brief account of his life and a rather damning critique of his work and himself, including dismissive claims, all unsupported by evidence, that 'he neither designed nor made the silver', that his drawings were 'by repute very primitive', that he was 'basically an entrepreneur' and that 'he never worked on a single piece himself'. The writer, Dr Peter Cannon – Brookes, was, as C. G. L. du Cann wrote two years later,'one of his [Ramsden's] most severe critics.'[2]

I felt it was time to re-open the case of Ramsden and Carr and when I began to talk with collectors, dealers, museum curators and others with an interest in silver or the Arts and Craft movement they all expressed an interest in knowing more about these silversmiths. I soon found that there was a great deal of misinformation about Ramsden and almost nothing was known of Carr. Only one photograph and one drawing of Ramsden were known and no image of Carr. There are very few of the usual primary sources of diaries or letters and neither man had any direct descendants, so where to begin?

A family portrait of Ramsden, aged 57, 1930.
(*Walt Ibbotson*)

Ramsden himself had had thoughts about gathering information on his work. Some of his correspondence with a regular client, from 1930 and 1931, shows that the lady in question had asked him if there was any existing collection of 'Literature' about his work. He replied:

> In answer to your query, there is a considerable amount of 'Literature' about my work, but it is scattered about in various periodicals and not easily obtainable.
>
> As a number of very kind clients have raised the point from time to time, I think I must see what can be done to collect and publish some sort of résumé, in which case it will give me pleasure to let you have a copy.[3]

This résumé was never made, so I decided to begin trying to collect something similar, albeit more than eighty years later.

Ultimately, the best sense of the strong convictions and character of Omar Ramsden came from two main sources; the texts of his many lectures and articles, and the previously unknown photographs of his studio and his family, on holiday and at leisure. Though I have uncovered photographs and a miniature portrait of Carr, I know of no written work by him, he seemed to prefer to keep out of the limelight. Possibly this was because when his business partnership with Ramsden ended, he went on to live with a male partner for the rest of his life. There is no evidence to suggest that Ramsden was gay. In 1895, when Carr was a young man of twenty-three, Oscar Wilde had been imprisoned for homosexual activity amid much scandal and publicity. This must have made for anxiety and watchfulness in a sensitive man like Carr. The document which has given me the best sense of Alwyn's character, his enduring affection for his partner Hughes, and his family relationships and interests, is his eleven-page last will and testament dated 1938. Reminiscences of the Hughes family suggest that they happily accepted the relationship between the two men, they have photographs of them together.

A miniature of Alwyn Carr, a copy was given to John Kelly by the Carr family.
(*Carr family*)

Early in my search, I met the (now retired) Librarian at the Goldsmiths' Company, David Beasley, who introduced me to the library archives, and to several people who lived and worked in the world of silver, previously quite unknown to me. David remembered correspondence with a Paul Hallam some years before, and I contacted him. Although very ill by then Paul was keen to share with me his information about Ramsden, now gifted to Goldsmiths' Archive. An ardent collector of Ramsden and Carr's work, he had spent years searching for details of their lives, mostly at a time before online research was possible. I was delighted that his family gave me the opportunity to study his collection of material on Ramsden and Carr before it went to the Goldsmiths Company, as he had bequeathed it. It includes several press cuttings which are undated and whose source is not noted. Where footnotes are lacking in my text, the source is one of those clippings, and no further information is available. It is worth remembering that Paul's notes and cuttings had been gathered purely for his own personal interest.

Another great step forward was tracing the grandchildren of Ramsden's wife, née Annie Emily Berriff. They gave a vivid picture of their grandmother Anne as a strong-minded and forceful woman. As well as talking freely about family matters, they very generously gave access to their collection of photographs, from about 1906 to 1960. They show Ramsden and Carr at the heart of Anne's family.

An advantage of twenty-first century research is the possibility of examining copies of certain original documents online. The General Register Office records of British Births, Deaths and Marriages, Wills and Census Returns make it possible to build up a picture of families and their backgrounds, occupations, aspirations and inter-relationships. Local Studies Libraries and Archives, particularly in Sheffield, provided many details of various kinds, such as Electoral Registers showing when and where people lived and commercial directories listing their businesses. Digitised newspaper archives are invaluable in exploring historical events and the tropes of a particular time. Anecdotes from members of related families fill out the detail.

Very soon I was completely engaged in the search and spent three years visiting the places where they studied, worked and lived, finding out as much as I could about the characters and lives of the two men behind the beautiful works of art marked 'Ramsden and Carr me Fecerunt'.

---

1 *Omar Ramsden, 1873–1939*, Birmingham Museum and Art Gallery, 1973. Introduction, Dr Peter Cannon-Brookes.

2 *Art and Antiques, Omar Ramsden – Silversmith and Salesman Extraordinary.* C. G. L du Cann, 19 July 1975.

3 Letter from Ramsden to Mrs Thornley, 28 October 1931, unpublished.

CHAPTER 1

Zeitgeist – Setting the Scene

Omar Ramsden and Alwyn Carr's creative lives developed from their deep interest in art, their friendship and their whole-hearted commitment to the success of their partnership. But it was also enabled by the prevailing ideologies and attitudes to commerce, art and craftsmanship of the world into which they were born. Their family backgrounds, their educational opportunities, the nature of manufacturing practices in their home city of Sheffield, contemporary ideas on the status of craft and design within art, and national developments in art and craft education, all played a part in their achievements.

On a local level, Sheffield in the 1870s was a teeming industrial centre for the manufacture of cutlery and metal work of all kinds. In the expanding town, designated a city in 1893, enterprising manufacturers could make fortunes, though their employees frequently fared much less well. Walker and Hall, Mappin and Webb, Lee and Wigfull, William Hutton and Sons are just a few of the well-known large firms that had vast premises and hundreds of employees. Picture Sheffield has an excellent collection of photos from that time, of the owners, the employees in the different sections of silver production, the workshops and the very elegant premises in London where the luxury goods were sold. Wealth was made through machine production of goods on an industrial scale. As far as decorative gold and silver was concerned, the resulting quality of machine made goods was much lower than that of work traditionally crafted by hand. As Ramsden was to say later, 'I got out of Sheffield as soon as I could, it was a city of manufacturers...' Ramsden and Carr's interest was in designing and making individual works by hand, in silver and other metals, it was to become the central tenet of their partnership.

View of Industrial Sheffield in 1854, by William Ibbit, 1854.
(*Sheffield Galleries and Museums Trust*)

Beyond their own city, the British Empire was thriving and bringing vast opportunities for world trade. The 1851 'Great Exhibition', or 'The Great Exhibition of the Works of Industry of all Nations' had been extremely popular and influential. In a fiercely competitive world market in manufactured goods the British government and industrialists were aware of the importance of quality of design. France and Germany already had well established training in technical arts; the first British Government School of Design had been formed in 1837, run by the Board of Trade to aid commerce. This evolved into the Department of Practical Art which in 1853 became the Department of Science and Art. This Department was later transferred to a new Education Department in 1856, giving a significant change in emphasis. It moved premises to the new South Kensington Museum (re-named the Victoria

Sheffield Buffer Girls, William Rothenstein, 1919.
(*Sheffield Galleries and Museums Trust*)

& Albert Museum in 1899) which took over its role. Its stated purpose was primarily educational; it aimed to reform and organise national training in art, crafts and design in order to improve manufactured products. It was not part of its remit to cover 'fine art', its interest was in commercial design and manufacture. Under its auspices, schools of design were set up in cities and towns in manufacturing areas. The Sheffield school had opened in a very small way in 1843 but was well established by the 1880s when Carr and Ramsden studied there. This background of national enthusiasm and support for education and training in arts and crafts had not been available to earlier generations, and without this opportunity it would have been much more difficult for Ramsden and Carr to progress as they did.[1]

As well as overseeing design schools and training standards, the South Kensington Museum acquired a first-rate collection of all the applied arts. Aspiring students were encouraged to learn and develop aesthetic judgement by looking at and drawing some of the finest objects in the world. As students in Sheffield, Omar and Alwyn were amongst those receiving financial help to allow them to do just this at South Kensington during their summer holidays.

Much nearer home in Sheffield, in 1875 the wealthy and famous John Ruskin, highly influential as an art critic, artist, political and social thinker, had opened a museum in Walkley, just half a mile from the Ramsden home in Fir Street and the Carr home in Freedom Road. Ruskin had founded the Guild of St George in 1871 in support of his social reforms. Searching for a suitable city to establish an educational museum for all, he had chosen Sheffield, partly because he was familiar with the natural beauty of the surrounding areas and also as he admired the skill of master craftsmen in the city's smaller metalworking shops. He thought he had an ideal curator in Henry Swan, who came from Sheffield. Swan was an engraver like many of the men in the Ramsden family, which would surely have encouraged them to visit. The Guild raised enough money to buy a house in Bell Hagg Road, Walkley. The museum opened in 1875, intended to be open to all comers, working men particularly, at times they would be able to visit. The collection was supplied by Ruskin, crammed into one tiny room thirteen feet square, the rest of the small house being occupied by Swan's family.

The founding of this small museum was directed to the aim of improving the artisan's life. The eclectic exhibits included drawings, books, copies of famous mediaeval paintings and geological and botanical specimens. The museum's purpose was to provide exhibits, free of charge, for the liberal education of the working man. The unusual objects of beauty and interest which were usually inaccessible to him meant that designs from nature and from the human hand could be closely observed, handled, enjoyed and copied. The museum attracted much interest nationally and locally. Janet Barnes quotes a letter which comments:

> ... in the museum are many things which prove to be charming in
> the eyes of the rough and hard workmen and we've not had a single
> instance of anything but the most pleasing and reverent attention –
> nothing approaching even the slightest degree to rude or flippant
> behaviour in them.[2]

The taste and dignity of the working man, for whom, unusually,
museum entry was often free, was considered to be improved by his
opportunity to view the excellent collections.

We know from his brother's notes that young Alwyn made 'constant
visits to the local art gallery at Weston Park and to the Ruskin Museum
then situated at Walkley Bank to satisfy his interest in art, artistic
expression and appreciation.'

From 1885, the Ramsden family were living in Walkley, so Omar
too had easy access to the museum, just ten minutes' walk from his
home. The Guild of St George has an early visitors book recording the
names and addresses of some of the museum visitors. Amongst them
are the young Omar, aged fourteen, and Alwyn's Aunt Anne Elizabeth
Ellison. Perhaps Omar visited with his father or uncles, all engravers.
They would have been just the kind of artisans for whom Ruskin had
founded the museum.

The 1891 census says that at the age of seventeen, Omar was an
'Assistant Teacher of Modelling, Board School, Silver Modeller,
Designer, Chaser, Engraver.' Board Schools were the first state schools,
set up by the 1870 Education Act, and they provided free education
to all children, compulsory to the age of ten. They were maintained
by local rates and run by local boards, hence the name. The Ruskin
Museum had just moved to Meersbrook Park where it was within easy
reach for all the students at the School of Art, where Omar attended
evening classes. Ruskin held that to study and copy the finest works
of art was crucial to the development of appreciation of good design.
Further, he viewed the system of industrial factory production which he

The museum visitors book showing Omar's signature, aged fourteen, 1887.
(*Guild of St George, Museums Sheffield*)

saw in cities everywhere as dehumanising to those within it. Not only
was it demeaning to the workers, but contributed to poor standards of
design and workmanship. Ruskin had a doubtless idealised view of the
Middle Ages as a better time for humanity, when craftsmen working
directly with their hands could have a satisfying relationship with their
work. His ideas were influential on William Morris, who is thought to
have visited the museum in 1886, and on C. R. Ashbee and other social
thinkers.

Janet Barnes quotes a letter sent to Walt Whitman in 1877 describing
contemporary Sheffield:

> I should like to describe to you the life of those great manufacturing
> towns like Sheffield. I think you would be surprised to see the squalor
> and raggedness of them. Sheffield is finely situated, magnificent hill
> country all round about, and on the hills for miles and miles (on one
> side of the town) elegant villa residences – and in the valley below one
> enduring cloud of smoke, and a pale-faced teeming population, and

tall chimneys and ash heaps covered with squalid children picking them over, and dirty alleys, and courts and houses half roofless, and a river running black through the midst of them. It is a strange and wonderful sight.[3]

Fortunately both Carr and Ramsden lived in happier conditions; Walkley at that time was a small village about two miles outside the city, accessible by tram. Barnes relates the position of the museum as described by a visitor in 1879:

> … the landscape it commands is a painter's dream of scenic loveliness. Built on the brow of a hill, the house overlooks the Rivelin Valley, or rather a series of converging valleys that in their wild and uncultivated beauty are suggestive of the Alps.

Ruskin's ideas on art, craft and social improvement were shared by William Morris, who viewed the huge expansion of capitalist manufacture, bringing wealth to the few, as demeaning to the majority who worked within it. What became known as the Arts and Crafts movement evolved from Ruskin and Morris's approach to design and craftsmanship as a social and political issue, rather than a specific design style within an artistic movement. Industrial production methods so divided and fragmented work output that there could be little satisfaction or pride in his task for the individual artisan. Mediaeval methods of hand production were seen as personally fulfilling to a skilled man, even if idealised by nineteenth century theorists.

Morris's view of the ideal of work was that designer and craftsman should be the same person. Accordingly, by 1875 he had established his firm of Morris and Company training men and women to hand make furniture, stained glass, wallpapers and a variety of textiles. His Kelmscott Press produced calligraphic work and illuminated manuscripts of great beauty. He created new typefaces evocative of mediaeval calligraphy, which Ramsden and Carr favoured for the quotations they often used on their work.

In his writings, including the Penny Pamphlets 'Monopoly, or How

Labour is Robbed', Morris advocated 'Useful work versus useless toil'. Influenced by Morris, C. R. Ashbee set up the Guild of Handicraft in the East End of London following similar principles, designing and producing fine works handmade by his craftsmen. The influence of his design ideas is evident in some of Ramsden and Carr's early silver. In time Ashbee moved his own and his craftsmens' families to the village of Chipping Campden in the Cotswolds where they could work in a healthy rural environment. They were successful for some years, but in practice the high cost of handmade goods meant that they were affordable only to the well-to-do. By 1908 the Guild was no longer financially sustainable and went into administration.

At that time Ramsden and Carr were establishing a successful partnership in London. The organisation of their own workshop was strictly on traditional lines, they were clearly in charge, whereas Ashbee had idealistically attempted to work on more democratic principles with his employees. Unlike Ramsden and Carr he might allow the marking of goods with an individual maker's name; in practice he was seldom involved in the making of pieces himself.[4] Unlike Ramsden, he was not criticised on this account. One has to say that Ramsden and Carr's methods proved ultimately more enduring and successful from a business point of view, though Ashbee was the finest of designers, highly imaginative and original.

Quality of materials, traditional methods of making, simplicity of design and freedom from superfluous ornament were central to the Arts and Crafts approach across a wide range of the applied arts: within architecture, furniture making, metalwork, jewellery, stained glass, textiles, calligraphy, glass, ceramics and tiles. Though many craftsmen and women espoused this approach and produced individual works of great beauty, inevitably such items have become collector's pieces or are held in museums, rather than being for the everyday use of the majority.

When it came to machinery, Ramsden and Carr seem to have trodden a path between working by hand and the occasional judicious use of machine tools. Their principles were concentrated on quality of design and materials and highest standards of workmanship rather than the wider social ideology of Ruskin, Morris and Ashbee. Their practical artisan backgrounds may have contributed to this; unlike the other men they did not have the backing of wealthy families or a public school and university education. Both had worked with their hands to earn a living in Sheffield, the heart of industrial production of silverware and metal work. They had won manufacturers' prizes for the design of commercial pieces and had 'been through the shops', though the passion of both was for the art of hand crafting. Their months in Europe and time in the South Kensington Museum, prior to setting up their own workshop, would have shown them examples of the finest work of craftsmen of all ages. This would have developed their intellectual appreciation of historical background and inspired and influenced them.

The degree to which use of machinery was acceptable within the Arts and Crafts movement was debated, many famous and respected names in the field used it in varying degrees. Mary Greensted noted that Walter Crane admired the technical skill and speed of the machine, Ernest Gimson used a minimum of machinery, Sidney Barnsley used a large circular saw in furniture making and designer W. A. Benson 'embraced mechanical production'.[5] Ramsden's own views were expressed in his talks, he was not necessarily against the use of machinery per se, although this attitude is often attributed to him by those who have not read his own words.

It seems that at some early stage, around 1908, the partnership did buy in readymade cigarette cases from Birmingham to keep their craftsmen working and to meet a keen demand for less costly items. Personal engraving and decoration could then be added for each client. The case which Alwyn Carr later gave his long-term partner Arthur Hughes is of this kind, with Hughes' initials engraved on the front yet having a Birmingham Hallmark. But that practice seems to have been brief, and not repeated, their work is generally known for its good weight of silver.

Ramsden and Carr, then Ramsden alone, kept the firm going and his craftsmen employed, even through the difficult trading years of the depression in the later 1920s into the 1930s when many businesses failed. Ramsden would have been aware of the need for careful management, having seen others meet with disaster. Ashbee was a gifted and original designer, with high ideals, but this had not prevented the collapse of his Campden enterprise and its consequences for the craftsmen who were put out of work. Several remained in the town and found other employment, but many had to return to London with their families. On a personal front, Ramsden was still living in the parental home when his father's business collapsed in 1896, bringing the shame of unpaid creditors and employees and the consequent breakup of the family. Charles Downs Butcher, whose family shared St Dunstan's Studio with Ramsden for years, saw his long-established textile business fail completely in 1927, leaving his widow penniless. Omar would have been very aware of the need to run any enterprise, however artistic and innovative, in a business-like way. He maintained a successful undertaking for forty years, producing work of the finest calibre and bearing the responsibility of keeping his craftsmen employed.

1 *Records of the Science and Art Department and Predecessors,*
    discovery.nationalarchives.gov.uk/details/rC810

2 *Ruskin in Sheffield,* Janet Barnes, Museums Sheffield, 1985. Revised Edition, Louise Pullen, 2011.

3 *Ruskin at Walkley: Reconstructing the St George's Museum,* Marcus Waithe,
    [http://www.ruskinatwalkley.org] [Accessed 10.05.2015]

4 *C. R. Ashbee, Architect, Designer and Romantic Socialist,* Alan Crawford, Yale University Press, 2005.

5 *The Arts and Crafts Movement in Britain,* Mary Greensted, Shire Publications, 2010, p9.

CHAPTER 2
Early Family Backgrounds

Omar was born in Sheffield on 21 August 1873, to Benjamin and Norah Ramsden. His birth certificate shows a few minor anomalies, his name being spelt as 'Omer', simply an error in spelling of a rather unusual name. His address is given as 16 Fir Street, though any search for it today would be in vain. The area near Sheffield is given as Nether Hallam, which included the ward of Walkley where he was born. Benjamin's occupation is given as 'engraver', and Norah's maiden name as Ibbotson.[1]

Why Omar? His rather exotic sounding name is often remarked upon, but it does not come from foreign ancestry, his ancestors were from Yorkshire for at least several generations. His mother Norah had six siblings, the youngest of whom was Omar Pasha Ibbotson. I think it safe to assume that she was particularly fond of this brother as she named her first son after him, though leaving out the 'Pasha'. For some time before her marriage in 1872, he and she lived alone together. Their parents had died, their older brothers had married and her only surviving sister had immigrated to the USA.

Why was her brother so called? In the year or two preceding his birth in early 1854, Omar Pasha of the Ottoman Empire seems to have been quite a hero in the eyes of the British. At this time a growing British public, probably including Omar Pasha Ibbotson's father George, were becoming avid newspaper readers. Communication and transport links were developing rapidly by 'electric telegraph', submarine and rail, bringing news of foreign affairs much more quickly than before.

There had been complex tensions throughout the nineteenth century between the Ottoman Empire – centred on present day Turkey – and Russia over territory and sea routes. Control of the Black Sea was crucial to profitable Western trade. Russia seemed to have designs on major parts of the Ottoman Empire from the Balkans through to Afghanistan and India. Religious differences between Russian Orthodox Christians and Turkish Muslims contributed to hostilities.

The commercial and political interests of the British, French and Ottomans as opposed to those of Russia, coincided for once and the British press was strongly anti-Russian, evident from newspaper archives of the time. Though without a natural affinity with the Ottomans, Britain found it useful to sympathise with their fight against Russian domination. More eminent Turks in powerful positions were viewed as sufficiently civilised and westernised to allow Britain to feel sympathy with their resistance to Russian bullying. Omar Pasha was one such Turk; 'Pasha', used after the first name was a title which could be granted to high ranking political or military men, suggesting 'leader'. Though now Turkish and Muslim, he had begun his military career in the army of the Austro-Hungarian Empire and so had some understanding of European practices and thought.

Against this background, his dashing military exploits caught the imagination of the British press. *The Times* made no less than 124 references to his activities in 1853, the year before 'our' Omar Pasha Ibbotson was born in January 1854. When the Turks formally declared war on Russia in October 1853, with the support of the British and French, Omar Pasha successfully led the hostilities.

On 11 October, *The Times* reported the instructions to Omar Pasha and others, they were to 'Be in readiness and prepared for all eventualities...'[2] Later that day came another report giving a brief summary of his life:

> The year 1851 was the most brilliant period of the military career of Omar Pasha... Commander in Chief of Bosnia. [He is] about 52 years of age, below the middle height but with a martial expression of countenance.

The battles and manoeuvres of the war were described in detail. It

Portrait of Omar Pasha, 1855.
(*Licensed under Creative Commons NCSA*)

seems probable that Omar Pasha Ibbotson's father George followed the reports closely and admired Omar Pasha's achievements, hence the decision to name his son after him. Other members in the family were named after heroic figures, including Livingstone and Gladstone. Although this cannot be proved it seems the most likely explanation for Omar Ramsden's name. Omar Pasha Ibbotson named his own son Omar Ibbotson in 1880 and the name has been passed down the generations from father to son. A third Omar was born in 1909, and R. Omar Ibbotson lives in Lincolnshire today.

One of the widely circulated 1973 'Ramsden myths' is that Alwyn Carr's family was 'considerably more prosperous than the Ramsdens and socially better placed'.[3] It has even been claimed that Alwyn came from an aristocratic family.[4] It is impossible to say where these rumours originated; census returns show that Alwyn's father was employed as a butcher throughout his life. Omar's parents were both from families who began life as artisans but made their positions financially sound. His Ramsden grandfather had become a middle-class professional, his Ibbotson grandfather had moved into Sheffield from a farming family who had lived in Dungworth, north-west of Sheffield, for several generations. He built up a successful business as an ivory cutter and trader, invested in property and land and was able to help his children financially. Both Omar's grandfathers were men with drive who made their own way in the world, both showed many of the characteristics which Omar was to develop.

Omar's father Benjamin, however, seems to have been financially less astute and less of a businessman than either his father or his son. He continually aspired to work on his own account but it seldom seems to have worked out well and he moved several times from self-employment to employment and back again, eventually failing completely.

Benjamin Woolhouse Ramsden had been born on 25 May 1850 at 20 Netherthorpe Place in Sheffield, the fourth of the six children of George, an Iron Moulder, and Eliza née Woolhouse.[5] George was ambitious from an early age; he joined the Oddfellows as a young man, eventually rising to Provincial Grand Master.[6] The Oddfellows is a Friendly Society, founded at least as early as the eighteenth century. It has affinities with the Freemasons, in that membership is organised through a system of local lodges, and their objectives included philanthropy and fraternity. The *Oddfellows Magazine*, of January 1871, has a glowing four-page article on George's life, with a detailed drawing of him:

> His parents were in humble circumstances, but it is no unmeaning phrase to say respectable; his father holding a post of considerable responsibility, but receiving a rather inconsiderable stipend, under a firm of wine merchants of high repute.

Over the years, George's father had been a labourer and a moulder, as well as working for the wine merchants. At fourteen, young George was put to an apprenticeship in his father's trade of stove grate moulder, in the firm of Yates, Haywood and Co., of Rotherham. By the age of seventeen he was already working diligently on behalf of the Oddfellowship and when he moved to Sheffield, due to 'his active habits, great intelligence, and genial temperament won the admiration and esteem of the Oddfellows'. He took on the responsibility of several offices and by 1871, the article states:

> Assuredly no member of the order has more richly deserved the high honour of the Grand Mastership than the sterling Oddfellow who now enjoys that distinction.

George applied the same dedication and energy to his career:

> It will be easily understood that, in those days of dear schools, the subject of this memoir could not get a classical training … but the thirst for knowledge was strong within him, and he continued, by close application in his leisure hours, so far to increase his scholarship, as to qualify himself for various offices of trust and responsibility – his present appointment in Sheffield being one which none but a quick arithmetician and a shrewd business man, could fill with any degree of satisfaction to the Town Council.

This was the position of District Rate Collector. The qualities above seem to be particularly like those which his grandson possessed; diligence, enthusiasm, capability, an interest in holding public office. Records show his involvement in such public affairs as managing claims after flooding in the city and improvements for Overseers of the Poor at the Crookesmoor Workhouse. On his own account, he was one of the earliest to take up the opportunity offered by the burgeoning Freehold Land Society movement to acquire a detached house on the desirable Birkendale Estate where Benjamin and his siblings were brought up. The original purpose of the scheme had been to give prudent members of 'the artisan classes' the opportunity to live away from their unhealthy work places in the city centre and 'migrate to the suburbs for healthful and remunerative exercise … and permanent residence.' The movement was widely adopted in Sheffield and the *Oddfellows* memoir describes his participation in the scheme:

> About this time a social reform engaged Mr Ramsden's attention. For some years building societies had been spreading, and at length the want of land whereon to build called for a remedy, and the first land society of which we have any knowledge was formed, having for its object the purchase of a large plot of land at Birkendale, Sheffield. Although Mr Ramsden was not one of the founders he early saw the great advantage of the system, and purchased a share in the Birkendale Freehold Land Society, and in a house erected on this very plot he has ever since resided.

Ida Villa, George Ramsden's house on the Birkendale estate where Omar's father was brought up, 2015. (*Author's photo*)

Membership of a Land Society scheme brought the opportunity to improve one's social and financial position, and both Omar Ramsden's grandfathers took advantage of it. House and land would be owned outright once the loan had been paid off, usually in fourteen years. Renting was the norm for most of the working population of the time, and of course continued into old age whereas a loan to buy would be paid off before retirement. Several estates were developed in the Walkley area, sometimes referred to as 'The Working Man's West End'. The Societies were part of the same wave of proposed social improvement for working men which had led John Ruskin to open his museum for them, also in Walkley, then a rural place on a hillside with open fields and extensive views, now completely built up. On Birkendale, where George Ramsden acquired his plot all the houses were larger than average, detached, on substantial plots, some with carriage houses, suggesting well-to-do owners. In spite of the scheme's original intentions their cost put them out of reach of even a skilled artisan in steady employment. The occupants were all of the middle class: Ramsden was the District Rate Collector, Honorary Secretary to the Birkendale View Society and Honorary Secretary to the local Steel Bank Bowling Green Society.

Birkendale is now a potentially very attractive Conservation Area, the mainly detached houses with large gardens being on a hillside with distant views. The streets have many of the original cobbles, street lamps, and mature trees. Houses currently vary between beautifully presented and maintained houses as they were in George Ramsden's time, and semi-derelict houses 'ripe for restoration'.[7]

George had married Eliza Woolhouse in 1844: they produced five sons and a daughter as they moved progressively upmarket to Ida Villa. But in 1866, when Benjamin was just 16, his mother died. George married again quite soon, producing another four daughters and a son, thus Omar had ten paternal aunts and uncles. All of the Ramsden boys served apprenticeships as engravers in the metal and cutlery trades for which Sheffield had long been famous.

On Omar's mother's side, many of the Ibbotsons were similarly entrepreneurial. His mother Norah was the daughter of another George and Eliza, née Driver, she and her brother Omar Pasha were the two youngest of eight. Their father moved from rural farm life into

Sheffield, became an Ivory Cutter and apprenticed his three sons to his trade.

Norah Ramsden, Omar's mother, undated. (*Walt Ibbotson*)

All became merchants, dealers and traders in ivory as well as cutters. George and his sons expanded their businesses over time, particularly Robert Ibbotson, whose firm became well known in Sheffield. A letter from him to his sister Elizabeth in the USA in 1893 says that he has 'a very heavy stock of Ivory and handles, nearly £20,000 worth.'[8]

Letter from Norah's brother Robert Ibbotson to their sister Elizabeth in the USA, 1893. (*Walt Ibbotson*)

Ivory was widely used at that time for all sorts of goods: for piano keys, billiard balls, jewellery, carved figures, decorative boxes, letter openers, penknives, handles for open razors and, especially in Sheffield, handles for good quality cutlery. Large firms had special departments for processing the ivory they needed, Joseph Rodgers & Sons are recorded as using twenty-four tonnes of ivory every year, using the tusks of 1,280 elephants, a harrowing statistic by today's standards. They employed five men exclusively for cutting.[9]

The current R. Omar Ibbotson has a postcard from Belgium dated 1919, just after the end of World War I. It was sent from Omar (the second) to his young son at home in Sheffield, (the third Omar) and advised him to tell his grandfather (Omar Pasha) to expect the price of ivory to be high. He wrote briefly of a Belgium devastated by war. At that time the Belgian Congo was a colony in Central Africa, (now the Democratic Republic of Congo) and a source of ivory, hence Omar Ibbotson's visit to Belgium. Although ivory was often sold by auction in London, he must have decided to go directly.

Postcard from war stricken Belgium, 1919, from Omar Ibbotson (2nd) to his son Omar. (*Robert Omar Ibbotson*)

As well as running his ivory business, Norah's father George Ibbotson bought and developed property, which was to be very helpful to Omar's parents later. Like Benjamin's father he too took advantage of the Freehold Land Society scheme and in 1849 bought land on the Fir View Estate large enough for six lots, building a house for himself on one of them.

He later divided the house into two, letting one of them for rent. The records are not very clear, but he certainly had an interest in producing an income from the building.[10] Norah was brought up in this house and spent much of her married life there; it was numbered as 16 Fir Street and is the house where our Omar was born. The present descendants think that George gave the house to his daughter Norah shortly before he died, when she became engaged to Benjamin. The houses were smaller than his Ramsden Grandfather's in Birkendale but both were owned by the family, and had 'One-Rood plots' (quarter acre) at the back for productive gardens. The photograph shows Norah, and Omar's brothers Wallace and Horace with their wives in the rear garden of 16 Fir Street in about 1929.

From left to right, Mamie, Horace, Dolly, Beatrice, Wallace, Norah seated, 1929.
(*Walt Ibbotson*)

Development within the schemes was very piecemeal, individuals bought plots but waited to build their houses as and when they could afford to. Thus houses were not built in straight terraces, and this could bring confusion and changes to house numbering. Walkley especially was dotted with houses, even today there are gaps in numbers in several streets.

In the 1860s George and his wife moved half a mile away to Bole Hill Lane, keeping the Fir Street houses in the family for the benefit of their children; the eldest son moved in with his family. In 1867 George felt comfortable enough at fifty-seven to retire, or 'decline business'. His stock of ivory was advertised for sale in the local paper.

George continued to invest in land, buying more at Bole Hill field. Unhappily, after only two years of retirement he died in 1869. Having started life as a labourer's son, at his death he was recorded as a 'gentleman' leaving something under £1,500. Some of his personal goods were advertised for sale at auction, including a 'DOG CART, in good condition; One-horse CART, set of GIG HARNESS…'

Much of his investment in land was kept in the family for several years; the family letter from Robert to Elizabeth Ibbotson twenty-four years later asked her if she wanted to sell her Bole Hill property. The implication seems to be that George left Bole Hill to his daughter Elizabeth and Fir Street to his daughter Norah.

George's widow died two years after him; Norah and her brother Omar Pasha lived together until Norah married Benjamin Ramsden in 1872. Her brother John, now an employer of several men and women, moved out of Fir Street to a much grander house, and Norah moved in, Omar was born there the following August.

Though both his Grandfathers were particularly enterprising men, Omar's father Benjamin had a rather restless working life, confirmed by trade directory entries. He first registered his own mark at the Sheffield Assay Office when he was twenty-two, at the Livingstone Works, Holly Street. In 1876, aged twenty-six, he was advertising in White's Directory, as a manufacturer rather than an engraver.

Three years later he was at 124 Rockingham Street as manufacturer of silver and electro-plate fish carvers, fish eaters, dessert spoons, knives, and scoops. But he must have thought there were better opportunities in the USA, as in 1879 he and Norah made the big decision to travel to the USA with Norah's older sister Elizabeth, her silversmith husband John Ibbotson and their two sons.[11] With six-year-old Omar they sailed from Liverpool to New York on the Britannic. He was incorrectly listed as Omah, a female aged four. Elizabeth and John Ibbotson had lived in Connecticut previously and must have spoken with enthusiasm of the opportunities there. Both families settled in Meriden, New Haven County, Connecticut, north east of New York, where the Ramsdens lived at 64 North Second Street. Benjamin was an engraver, Omar was at school.[12] Two years later Omar's brother Wallace was born, and an unsubstantiated family story says that there was another child who died. Norah's sister and her husband seem to have gone backwards and forwards over the Atlantic several times, they have many descendants in the USA today.

Both sisters named their first sons after their closest brother, Norah after her brother Omar, Elizabeth after her brother Robert; there is more than one photo of Elizabeth and Robert before both married, as well as the letter from him to her when they were much older. This son Robert was back in Sheffield in 1896, when he married Minnie Mellor. The Ramsdens and Ibbotsons gathered for a party in August to say goodbye to them before their return to the USA. Both Omar and Alwyn, who had met as students at the School of Art, went to the party and did quick sketches of Minnie as tokens of farewell, the earliest known examples of their drawings (see pages 34 and 35).

Robert's grandson Walt Ibbotson has these sketches today, and is custodian of a large collection of early photographs, documents, mementoes, letters and certificates relating to the Ibbotson family. There are photos of Omar's mother Norah, some of her siblings, their father George, and some of Omar's many cousins. What persuaded the young Ramsdens and Ibbotsons to undertake the long journey to Meriden? The city had been developing silver manufacturing processes since the early 1800s. Connecticut had thriving companies making silverware, particularly silver plate and electro plate, for which there was a growing middle-class market for whom it was much more affordable than sterling silver. One of the most important and long-lived firms was the Wallace Company, is it fanciful to imagine that Benjamin named his American born son after them?

The *Meriden Daily Reporter* of 2 January 1891 has advertisements for at

alwyn&barr
1896
sheffield

Oh Lady, passing to some
other land to dwell.
I wish a happy life,
and all that's well.

Above and right: Sketches by Omar and Alwyn, made at a family party, 1896.
(*Walt Ibbotson*)

least half a dozen companies manufacturing silver and electroplate in the town. For example, the Meriden Cutlery Company advertised table cutlery and claimed exclusive use of a patent for celluloid handles. Like many other companies they had factories in Meriden and showrooms in major cities in North America and London.

It seems highly probable that in this period of rapid growth these businesses sought skilled men from British manufacturing centres like

An advertisement in the 'Meriden Daily Reporter', 1891.
(*www.silvercollection.it*)

Sheffield. A page of a Federal Census for the Ibbotsons' neighbourhood shows many of the same occupations as in the Sheffield cutlery and metal trades, including a Britannia worker, a chaser, a cutlery finisher, a cutlery inspector, an etcher, metalwork day labourers, a handle finisher, a silver plater, an augur polisher, a spoon tinner and a scissors burnisher. Benjamin had been an engraver in England and would have had useful skills and experience in the trade, so should have found employment easily. He is recorded as working for two major firms in Connecticut, C. Rogers and Brothers, and Manning, Bowman and Co., both had branches in Chicago, which could explain why some of the family think the Ramsdens went to Illinois in 1882 or 1883, but there does not seem to be any evidence of this. What records there are, show the family settled in Meriden, and Omar attended school there.

The rate books show that both their Fir Street houses were let, so however the sojourn abroad worked out, they did have a house to return to. While they were away Fir Street was renumbered so that number 16 became 70, and number 14 became 68, as they are at present.

Wallace, the second son, was born in the USA but the family was back in Fir Street by 1885 when the third son Horace was born. By 1887 Benjamin was again employed, this time as a manager in a cutlery firm. Omar was fourteen and old enough to be apprenticed as his father and uncles had been. It has been claimed that this was with his father, but as Benjamin did not have a business of his own then, he was not in a position to enter into apprenticeship agreements. Possibly Omar was taken into the firm his father worked for; this was not uncommon for the sons of employees. The *Weekly News* of October 1899, describing the presentation of the Sheffield mace which Omar designed, says that Omar was 'put to a firm of Sheffield silversmiths' in 1887, at fourteen, the usual age for apprenticeships to start. He remained in the city for ten more years and would have received a solid grounding in aspects of silver production on a large scale. He later said he valued this, even though it was not the way he wanted to progress. In 1888, he started evening classes at Sheffield School of Art.[13]

Norah's three brothers, Robert, John and Omar Pasha were small employers with one or two domestic servants and nursemaids. They had fifteen children between them, and all their sons went into the ivory business. Thus, Omar came from a family which was large by any standards, with seventeen aunts and uncles, at least nineteen Ramsden cousins, fifteen Ibbotson cousins living locally plus a few in the USA. Alwyn, on the other hand, had two maiden aunts so no cousins on his mother's side and if there were any on his father's side I have been unable to find any trace of them. Of his two brothers, one produced two children, altogether a much smaller family.

Contrary to the claims of the 1973 catalogue that Alwyn Carr's family was socially much superior to the Ramsdens, the fact is that his father Charles Carr was employed as a butcher from at least the age of sixteen. He stayed in that trade until he retired, his homes were modest and he left very little money when he died.[14] He married as a young man and the couple had a daughter, but after the early death of his first wife he married Emily Ellison. They produced three sons, the first was born in August 1872 and named Alwyn Charles Ellison Carr. Two brothers followed, William Hinchcliffe and Arthur. The three boys spent several of their early years in a cottage near Hukin Farm, Elm, north of Sheffield. The Ordnance Survey map of 1905 shows that even then it was a sparsely populated rural area called Sheffield Lane Top, scattered with a few farms and large houses.[15] At the time it was near the hamlets of Shire Green and Wincobank, an area now completely built up. These early rural years probably encouraged in Alwyn the love of the countryside that he kept for the rest of his life. In *Who's Who* of 1936 he named long country walks as one of his recreations. Attending Pitsmoor National School, he must have appeared bright and able, as instead of leaving at fourteen in the usual way, he went on to Sheffield Central Higher Grade School for a further three years.

His brother Arthur later related how the art master, Mr Fanshawe, was a great influence on Alwyn:

[His] sympathetic attitude, encouragement and stimulative [sic] teaching aroused his interest in Art and fostered his latent artistic talent. Art, artistic expression and appreciation became a passion which he sought to satisfy even at that early age by constant visits to the local Art Gallery at Weston Park, Sheffield, and to the Ruskin Museum, then situated at Walkley Bank as well as by tentative sketching expeditions and rambles among the beauties of the neighbouring Rivelin Valley.[16]

After some years Alwyn's father left the farm for the town and lived above the butcher's shop which he managed at 222 Grimesthorpe Road, a long road of modest terrace houses opening straight onto the pavement, now demolished. Their immediate neighbours in 1891 included several labourers in local industries, and a charwoman next door. There is no evidence of considerable prosperity, although a butcher with regular access to meat probably fared well compared to other artisans when it came to feeding his family.[17]

Alwyn's mother Emily was the daughter of Charles Ellison, his father was Joseph Ellison, of whom there was a family portrait. Alwyn mentioned this portrait specifically in his will, leaving it to his nephew. This possession of a family portrait is the only suggestion of middle-class prosperity that I can find. Emily's father Charles was a filesmith for most of his life; by 1881 he was recorded as a File Manufacturer, but it must have been in a small way, as was often the case in this trade. He lived for

years at 70 Freedom Road (now re-numbered 114) with his wife Sarah and three daughters Ann, Emily and Clara.

70 Freedom Road (now 114) where Alwyn lived with his Aunts Ann and Clara Carr, 2015. (*Author's photo*)

Ann, a school mistress, was also one of the early signatories of the Visitors Book in the new Ruskin Museum in 1880. The youngest sister Clara was a milliner, and Alwyn's mother Emily was the only daughter to marry. She married widower Charles Carr when she was thirty.

Alwyn's grandfather Charles achieved local notoriety when in early 1873 'serious complaints' were made against him, it was alleged that he 'had grossly neglected his duty'. Retired from filesmithing, he was a collector of voting papers on an important local concern. He had taken it upon himself to advise several voters to destroy some of their papers. The Mayor judged that it:

> Was no business of the collectors whether the voting papers were filled up or not and they had no right … to influence the vote. In answer to these charges Ellison made several incoherent statements… but gave no satisfactory explanation of his conduct. [The Mayor] did not believe he had been criminal in his intentions, but he did not think he was a proper person to be entrusted with voting papers.[18]

By the time of the 1891 census, eighteen-year-old Alwyn had left his parents' home to live with his unmarried aunts in Freedom Road. He was employed as a 'Modeller and Designer' which suggests that he, like Omar, worked in the silver trade. He had been taking evening classes since 1888, but had not yet won the scholarship which allowed him to be a full-time student. By coincidence Freedom Road was only a five-minute walk away from the Ramsden home in Fir Street, so it seems probable that the two young men became friendly at their evening art classes and travelled home together on the tram to Walkley. Their shared passion for art and creativity, with their hopes and ambitions for the future must have cemented their friendship.

Seventeen-year-old Omar was also showing talent. He was teaching at the Board School, but it is possible this was only part-time, or perhaps he did not complete the usual seven-year apprenticeship. Either way, he was industrious and hard-working.

His father Benjamin, however, seems to have been unable to

settle into working for anyone else. In 1893, records in the Sheffield Assay office show that he was now at 245 Rockingham Street as an engraver. He was obviously inventive, he was granted a patent in 1895 for 'Creating an Improvement in the Tanging of Cutlery and Other Articles.' Tanging is the means by which the projecting part of a knife blade is firmly fixed within the handle, which may have been bone, ivory, metal or celluloid.[19]

Although he was brought up in comfortable circumstances by an entrepreneurial father, and showed artistic and inventive talents, the ability to run a successful business in difficult times seems to have eluded Benjamin, and these qualities passed directly from grandfathers to grandson, missing out Benjamin. The financial difficulties which his father experienced must have influenced Omar as a young man and convinced him of the need to make sure his own enterprise was run well.

Unfortunately, in 1896 Benjamin's business failed completely, he was forty-six. As *The London Gazette* shows, he was unable to pay his creditors.[20] It may have been that he just did not have the right character to be an entrepreneur, but in any case the late 1890s were difficult times in the Sheffield cutlery trade as Robert's letter confirms; foreign competition, tariffs in the USA which the letter refers to, increasing mechanisation and the development of stainless steel all contributed to a general decline. It seems likely that Benjamin's pride suffered badly. It would have meant shame and humiliation in an area where he was well known. To make the situation worse, this was a year when his son Omar was doing particularly well at the art school, receiving local acclaim and praise for his commission to design the city mace. Soon after the bankruptcy, Benjamin went back alone to the United States where he had worked formerly, and after a few years seems to have disappeared entirely.

Norah's father's shrewd investment in property meant that the Fir Street houses could be rented out to provide her with an income. They were not lost in the bankruptcy, probably because they were registered in her own name, having come from her father. In time, she moved with her two younger sons to a small shop which she ran herself. Wallace, at nineteen, was a gold and silversmith and candlestick maker, Horace was fifteen and Omar had moved to London.

By 1899 the Meriden City Directory showed Benjamin working for C. Rogers & Brothers. Again, he appears unsettled, moving from Olive Street to Main Street to Hanover Street and going from job to job. The next year he was employed by Manning, Bowman & Co., later as a metal solderer for C. R. Brothers of Cheshire Street. This seems to be the same firm as C. Rogers and Brothers; although they were absorbed in time into larger businesses they kept their trademark '1847 Rogers Brothers' for many years, as a sign of quality.

In the 1900 US Census Benjamin gave his state as 'married', although he and Norah were living apart. This is the last record anywhere of his whereabouts, in spite of extensive searches by family and professional genealogists. In 1903 Omar's brother Wallace went to the USA, probably encouraged by the Sheffield family to find out how Benjamin was faring. He was twenty-one, had enough money to pay his own fare and economised by travelling in steerage. The shipping document indicates that he had $100 with him, more than any other of the steerage passengers. His father is named as B. W. Ramsden of Meriden, and they may or may not have met, but in any event Wallace returned to England without him, and no traces have been found since.

He seems to have vanished, and this probably led to the rumour that he had set up another unofficial family, possibly under a different name. There were so many of his wife's Ibbotson family in Connecticut that he probably kept it very quiet if it was true; none of the descendants has any evidence to offer. Norah was still declaring herself as 'married' rather than widowed in 1911, implying that Benjamin was alive although he was not with her. When Horace married in 1912 he stated that his father was a silversmith, the implication again being that he was still alive, but not necessarily so. If a bridegroom's father was dead the word 'deceased' was often, though not always, added to the certificate after his occupation was given.

1 England and Wales BMD Birth Index, 21 August 1873, Ecclesall Bierlow, West Riding
2 'Latest Intelligence', *The Times* [London, England] 11 Oct 1853: 6. *The Times Digital Archive* Web, 1 March 2016
3 Birmingham 1973
4 *Apollo 75* 1961: p184 Eric Delieb
5 BMD Birth Index, 25 May 1850, Sheffield, West Riding
6 *Oddfellows Magazine*, January 1871, PHA
7 https://www.sheffield.gov.uk/.../conservation/conservation-areas/birkendale...
8 Letter from Robert Ibbotson to his sister Elizabeth, 29 Dec 1893, unpublished.
9 Exhibits, Department of Metalwork, Museums Sheffield.
10 Rates books and Electoral Registers.
11 *New York Passenger Lists, 1820–1957, Britannic*, 25 August 1879.
12 9 June 1880 US *Federal Census*, Meriden, New Haven.
13 *School of Art Record Book*, Sheffield, 1888–1898, The Special Collection, Adsetts Library, Hallam University.
14 England and Wales Census, 1851, Yorkshire, Brightside Bierlow
15 Ordnance Survey Map, 1905, Yorkshire West Riding, Sheet CCLXXXVIII.II.
16 *Notes on Captain Alwyn C. E. Carr,* 16 November 1940. Unsigned, though probably by Carr's brother Arthur. Copy in Museums Sheffield, Department of Decorative Arts.
17 England and Wales Census 1891, Sheffield.
18 *Sheffield Independent*, 16 January 1873.
19 UK Patent 18940807-A 2014directorypatent.com
20 *London Gazette*, 9 June 1896, p3413

CHAPTER 3
Sheffield School of Art

Records of the School of Art and local newspapers show that Omar and Alwyn studied there for approximately ten years, beginning around September 1887 and leaving in June 1897. It would seem that at first both studied part-time at evening classes while working during the day, until awarded full Sheffield Corporation scholarships which provided them with enough money to devote themselves to full-time study. The school was recognised as one of the highest achieving in the country by the Department of Science and Art in South Kensington, which oversaw competition between about one thousand schools of art in the country. Both young men studied and practised a wide range of skills, which gave them a sound basis in drawing and design for the rest of their lives. The traditional courses were Drawing from Life, Drawing from the Antique, Drawing Historic Ornament, Principles of Ornament, Model Drawing, Freehand Drawing, Shading from the Cast, Modelling and possibly others. No classes in practical work were offered in the earliest days of the college, but were added over the years.[1]

The School of Design in Sheffield opened in 1843, evolving into the Sheffield School of Art and then into the present Hallam University over the next one hundred and fifty years. The first premises consisted of a modest rented room within the Bath Saloon, Victoria Road, which comprised the whole school. To begin with, classes were offered in the early mornings or in the evenings after 6.30pm, so that working people could attend before or after their day's work, which may have been as long as ten hours. Daytime classes were for gentlemen, ladies and amateurs, with male and female classes being kept strictly separate at first.[2]

The Sheffield School of Art was the third of many set up nationally by the government, their purpose was to increase the profitability of businesses, not to encourage 'artists'. The Government Board of Trade, local councils and manufacturers provided funding, and schools were managed locally but under the ultimate control of the national Department of Science and Art. Their original stated purpose was to train men and women with artistic flair in order to upgrade the design and manufacture of British goods for a competitive market. 'Fine' art was not to be offered as a subject for study, courses were intended to be strictly confined to those useful for commerce.

I found the first mention of Carr and Ramsden's activities in the School of Art in the *Sheffield and Rotherham Independent* of 27 September 1888, in a report on the school's annual achievements. Aged fifteen and sixteen, both were mentioned for their grades in freehand drawing and modelling, Omar additionally received a prize as his drawing was rated 'first class'. The attitude of the report writer towards useful training is very apparent in his remarks:

> … it is satisfactory to notice that a very large proportion of the awards are for works that are strictly technical and applied to the art trades of Sheffield, that the school is carrying out the objects for which it is founded and is not degenerating into the un-useful. The committee of the school requires it to be conducted on such lines as will be most useful to the practical art workman and to the manufacturer.[3]

By the time of the 1890 report, arrangements were being put into place for practical work, in the form of a large new studio for wood carving and modelling. Both young men received annual prizes, and work by Carr was accepted towards a teaching certificate, then and in following years; perhaps he was considering a future career. The annual address by the headmaster was very strongly worded, he quoted 'a well-known truism':

> The artistic quality of a nation's manufactures and its prosperity through the applied arts, depends on the high level of excellence in the fine arts. But it is found that there is a point at which the high level of excellence in the fine arts ceases to exert its influence for

good on the nation's manufactures, or to raise the artistic quality of the applied arts.

Mr J. T. Cook continued, blaming well-meaning people for:

Encouraging young men to do nothing but paint pictures or works which are altogether non-industrial. The picture mania is nothing but an unhealthy craze which affects a large number of the well-to-do inhabitants of this country and which practically forces young men into the ranks of the mediocre picture painters.

He exhorted the public to:

Agitate for works something similar to those seen at the Arts and Crafts Exhibition in London; and to acknowledge the fact that the ivory carver, the chaser, modeller and engraver...has quite as much brains, and an equal chance of showing it as the ordinary picture painter.

He was reiterating the ongoing argument which had encouraged the formation of the Art Workers Guild two years previously, namely, for the perception of designer/craftsmen as professionals rather than merely artisans.

Despite various decrees from London the curriculum did widen in time to include the fine arts of drawing, painting and sculpture, and in due course the Sheffield School of Design became the Sheffield School of Art. A major step forward was made when the school began to offer full-time courses as well as those geared to employed artisans, it meant that talented students who could afford it were able to concentrate fully on practice and study. Sheffield Corporation gave full scholarships of £52 for one especially gifted advanced student from each year; both Carr and Ramsden were granted them. The newspaper reported in 1896 that Alwyn received the only fourth year student scholarship and Omar received the only third year one.[4]

The art school also set up classes in local board schools for young pupils, at first for the teaching of drawing, and by Omar's time for such crafts as woodcarving, embroidery, bookbinding and metalwork. By 1891 he was one of those providing such instruction. Aged only seventeen he was already considered able enough to be an Assistant Teacher at a Board School though he did not attain an official Complete Art Class Teacher's Certificate until later.

The local paper continued to publish the art school's reports over the years. During Omar and Alwyn's time as students the annual end of year gathering was visited by the Director of the South Kensington Museum. Comments were made on how William Morris, Walter Crane and others had spoken highly of the work of Sheffield students. Carr's 'very clever model of the dock leaf' was singled out with a special mention.

The year ending June 1893 saw a special celebration of the 50th anniversary of the founding of the school, and was fortunate in securing Walter Crane's attendance at the event. He was a highly influential figure in the Arts and Crafts world and an internationally renowned painter, writer on design, and illustrator. It was agreed that the Sheffield School of Art had become a school of the first rank winning many of the highest national awards. Prizes included payments of tuition fees for:

> Youths of the artizan [sic] class, aged 12 to 17, who are or intend to be apprenticed to some of the staple traders of the town, tenable at evening classes for seven years.

Both Omar and Alwyn were awarded these although they were over seventeen, and it was questionable whether they intended their futures to be with 'the staple traders of the town'.[5]

The President was glad to see the eminence given to design and handicraft, and he, like many in the ongoing debate, saw no essential difference between fine art, decorative art and industrial art. After the report came the 'Conversazione', a scholarly social gathering for the discussion of art and literature. Walter Crane gave the address and distributed prizes, including awards to Omar and Alwyn. The distinguished Crane was an early Master of the Art Workers Guild, to which Omar and Alwyn were later invited to membership. In 1888, he had been president of the 'Arts and Crafts Exhibition Society' when they held their first exhibition. This was the first time the phrase 'Arts and Crafts' had been used to denote an approach to art and certain characteristics of style. Later in his career Ramsden produced beautiful silver book-mounts for books illustrated by Crane, one of which is now in the Wilson Museum, Cheltenham.

At the prize-giving Crane said that he had a long association with the area, having spent many hours painting the local countryside in the open air: 'In old days he found his best school of art within a few miles of that place, among the hills of Derbyshire and on the banks of the Derwent'.

This Jubilee year ending 1893 was the first in which Alwyn received his full scholarship of £52 for his excellent results in national examinations; he continued to receive it in the four following years. The examiner also noted that in national competition: 'The full number of marks has been awarded to the models by Omar Ramsden of Sheffield School of Art for a very interesting design remarkably well treated'. He was mentioned once more in this same report for his 'very exceptional ability'.

Even at twenty and twenty-one, the abilities of the two young men were recognised; they were bringing credit to the school. Awards directly from South Kensington were through national competition, '...to those Students who execute the most meritorious of the Works...' National awards included those which paid for winners to attend a two-week course of lectures at South Kensington during the summer vacation. In 1896 Alwyn, Omar, Millicent and Eleanor Mercer and Edward Wigfull (see following) all won them, so it seems probable that they went to London together. Their examiners had included members of the Royal Academy and such luminaries of the art world as William Morris, William de Morgan, W. R. Lethaby, Walter Crane and Sir Hamo Thornycroft RA, whose former studio was later to become Alwyn's London home. The talent and promise of the young students was being recognised and developed, they were fine examples of the way in which Ruskin's ideals were being put into practice.

National book prizes, medals and awards came the way of the young men during every year of study. Omar took a Queen's prize for exceptional ability in 1896. It would be tedious to list every award of both young men, only a selection is mentioned here, but all are detailed in the Sheffield School of Art Reports Book.

It was customary for local businessmen to make awards, usually for designs useful to Sheffield manufacturers. In 1896 Omar received special mention in the Headmaster's Report, reproduced as usual in the *Sheffield and Rotherham Independent*:

> Omar Ramsden has highly distinguished himself this year in the examinations by obtaining two prizes for special Excellence in Advanced work. The Department's Examiner ... on reporting on his design for an electric bell, says: 'It is perhaps the best example of good and distinctive treatment of two materials. The panel, bronze, and the mouldings, stone, are perfect treatments of both materials while at the same time they are so well designed together that the one enhances the other in the highest degree.[6]

Examples from major manufacturers in the city confirm Omar and Alwyn's dedication and talent. Messrs Martin, Hall and Co. awarded a five guinea prize to Omar for the best design for a six-cup egg-stand and spoons. From Messrs William Hutton & Sons, Ltd. came a £25 prize for his design for a tea and coffee service, a very large sum for the time.

Mr Henry Wigfull gave a more modest drawing prize of two guineas. He was a local businessman who built up the successful firm of Lee and Wigfull, employing fifty men and fifty women. His firm manufactured silver and electroplated ware which is still collected. Picture Sheffield has an excellent collection of early photographs of some of these manufacturers, their workers and premises. W. Edward Wigfull, Henry's nephew, was a fellow student of Omar and Alwyn, and they later all lived as neighbours in the Albert Studios in Battersea.

The Sheffield Master Cutler's Prize of five guineas went to Alwyn in 1896 for the best design for a modelled panel for the back of a dog stove, suitable for casting in iron and bronze. Possibly this is the one illustrated in the copy of *The Artist* of 1902, which reviewed several Ramsden and Carr works made in different metals: a wrought iron fire casket, some handsome door furnishings and a hanging lamp.[7] Three of the pieces incorporate versions of the winged hammer device which the pair used jointly and separately for many years. Thirty years later in 1928 Ramsden was to be commissioned to make presentation pieces for the same Master Cutlers.

Also in 1896 Mr H. L. Brown presented Omar with the first prize for the Model of a Ceremonial Key in Wax. This has survived, though now very fragile, and is carefully preserved in its case in the Adsetts Special Collection. It was taken to be X-rayed in 2013 and its inner metal strengthening structure was revealed. The model may be Omar's first exhibited work. The key was accepted for the 1897 Spring Exhibition at the prestigious Leeds City Art Gallery, together with a 'Casket Suitable for Containing the Freedom of a City or an Address' and a repoussé head in copper. [8] This was the first of many times Ramsden was invited to exhibit in Leeds. Over the next thirty years his work was shown there alongside decorative art and paintings by such famous names as C. R. Ashbee's Guild of Handicrafts, James Powell Glass, now Whitefriars, Arthur Rackham, William Rothenstein and the Ruskin Pottery. Throughout the 1920s and 30s the gallery also held Yorkshire Artists Exhibitions, confined to those who had a connection to a Yorkshire art school.[9]

In their final year of study Omar did particularly well, Alwyn just a little less so. The competition between the two must have been close and intense, if friendly. Omar nearly always just had the edge over his fellow student in terms of awards and grades. For example, in this last year Omar achieved first class in Drawing from the Antique, Alwyn achieved second class. Omar was awarded an excellent grade for Drawing Historic Ornament, Alwyn second class. In Principles

Wax model of a key, made by Ramsden while a student, 1896.
(*Adsetts Special Collection, Hallam University, Sheffield*)

of Ornament both were designated first class. In Model Drawing, Advanced, Omar was awarded first class, Alwyn second; in Freehand Drawing Omar was excellent, Alwyn first class. In 'Shading from the Cast', both achieved first class.

Later comment from the 1973 catalogue mentioned earlier, implying that Omar was merely brilliant as 'an actor and salesman' and that Alwyn and others carried out all the drawing and designing seem completely unfounded given these records, as well as the many contemporary reviews in prestigious art journals throughout their working lives.

The Studio published a long article in September 1896 about the problems of the National Competitions of South Kensington, to which Omar and Alwyn had both submitted work. It seems that 88,854 items had been sent there from art schools in the hope of an award. J. W. Gleeson-White, the editor and writer, wrote of:

> The usual mood that depresses the annual critic – the hopelessness born of experience that makes him dread the duty ... Who needs the nth repetition of an acanthus scroll...? There are some teachers who fail to see that it is the letter only which is teachable, and that too great insistence upon the letter kills the spirit.

Happily, Gleeson-White judged that this year things had improved, 'the tedious mechanical stuff is in so small a minority that it ceases to be apparent'. Several pages evaluating the submitted works followed: book illustration, tiles, invitation cards, embroideries, and a wide range of arts and crafts. Omar was mentioned for a casket design, 'to be worked in silver, apparently'. It was 'very new in its form and full of graceful detail' and was one of the few selected for illustration.[10]

While at the School of Art, Omar and Alwyn were friends and colleagues with several fellow students with whom they remained in touch. On visiting Sheffield to study their records of the time, and reading through the long lists of students in the Art School Report of 1897 I came across the name of Wallace Ramsden, Omar's younger brother, then aged fifteen. He too must have had some artistic talent, as he attained a first-class grade in Model Drawing and a second class in Modelling. He became a silver and goldsmith in England and later the United States, where he made a good living, though he was never in his brother's league.

Searching through dozens more pages of students' names over a five-year period the name of Albert Edward Ulyett (pronounced Yoolett I believe) caught my eye when, aged sixteen, he achieved a second-class grade for Elementary Freehand Drawing. The next year he won a council prize of ten shillings for achieving first class grades in two

A front cover of 'The Studio Journal', 1893. (*Out of copyright*)

elementary examinations and the next year, 1897, a second class in the Principles of Ornament. The familiar name was indeed the same person who worked for Ramsden and Carr in London for many years, eventually becoming the trusted manager of the workshop in Maxwell Road. Their time at the school overlapped, though he was a few years younger than them. He too had been born in Sheffield where his father Edwin was a groom and coachman.

W. Edward Wigfull was a student contemporary with Omar and Alwyn from at least 1892 to 1897. He too received several awards, noted in the art school records, primarily for design and drawing. His uncle Mr Henry Wigfull, manufacturer of silver and electroplate, was mentioned above as a donor of student prizes. With his brother Joshua, Edward also left Sheffield for London and by 1901 Omar and Alwyn were in adjoining studio premises near Albert Bridge with him, his brother and others, in a row of very pretty purpose-built artists' studios. Edward became an illustrator; his best-known commissions included the illustration of stories by Percy Westerman, voted the best writer of boys' adventure stories in the 1930s, now highly collectible. A keen amateur yachtsman, Edward often wrote for *Yachting Weekly*; in 1914, he wrote an amusing illustrated article, 'Round About Canvey,' which can be seen online. Posters of some of his paintings are still reproduced, he was another of Omar and Alwyn's successful co-students.

Millicent and Eleanor Mercer likewise studied with Omar, Alwyn and Edward for most of their years at the Sheffield School of Art, achieving the same awards which paid for them all to go on summer courses at South Kensington. Through their mother Louise Emerson, the sisters were distant cousins of the famous American author, Ralph Waldo Emerson. It seems quite probable that they stayed in contact with Ramsden and Carr, and possible that Millicent did some work for them.

Eleanor was a particularly talented artist silversmith, winning prizes and scholarships of all kinds, plus two gold medals and books. 'First class' and 'excellent' commendations for drawing and design were scattered liberally throughout her work at the school. Contrary to another of the Ramsden myths she was the only one of the group to win a full scholarship of £105 in 1895 to study at South Kensington for a full year. The Lady's Pictorial wrote an article on her in 1896, saying:

> She is exactly the type of student for whose benefit and instruction the Government's School of Design was originally promulgated. Miss Mercer began doing chasing and repoussé work in 1885 in the room provided by the Yorkshire Ladies Council of Education…

Her work was exhibited at the Royal Academy and the Metropolitan Museum in New York has her signed graphite drawing of a door-knocker in the Arts and Crafts style. Like Ramsden and Carr, in 1904 she had her work fully appraised in *The Studio*. The family story from Con Mercer, great-grandson of her brother, relates how her exquisite work was on permanent display in the Mappin and Webb showrooms in Oxford Street until the premises were destroyed by wartime bombing. Unfortunately, Eleanor suffered from consumption and although she went to South Africa to stay with her brother Louis hoping for an improvement in health, her particularly promising career was cut short by her death there in 1900 at the age of twenty-nine. Mappin and Webb had large manufacturing works in both Sheffield and in London and a reputation for quality goods. Sheffield Local Studies Library has several fascinating catalogues showing employees working in different specialisms at the works, and their goods in the palatial showrooms in London where Eleanor's work was displayed.

Millicent, her younger sister was another co-student of Omar and Alwyn, winning several awards, though not in the same exceptional category as her sister. Circumstantial evidence suggests that Millicent may have worked in London at some time for Ramsden and Carr. Records show that by the age of sixteen she was already working in Sheffield as a chaser in silver and gold. In 1909 aged about thirty four, she made a silver bowl very much in the Ramsden and Carr Arts and Crafts style, signing it in the form invariably used by the partnership then, *Millicent Mercer Me Fecit Dec MCMIX* as though in acknowledgement of a relationship with them. Yet the sponsor's or maker's mark is that of William Gallimore, a Sheffield maker. When Alastair Dickenson showed me this beautiful dish, we could only speculate on how this interesting association might have come about.

In 1901 in the early days of Ramsden and Carr's partnership Millicent was living near them in Fulham Road with her author sister Caroline, employed as a designer and chaser. The 1911 census shows her still employed as a silver chaser working for un-named employers who were 'Art Metal Workers', could it have been Ramsden and Carr? She lived then just off the Fulham Road with her brother Arthur, still under half a mile from the Maxwell Road workshop. She never registered a mark of her own and there is no evidence that, unlike Eleanor, she worked on her own account. Ramsden and Carr put their joint mark on every piece that left their workshop, as was the usual practice, regardless of who had contributed to its making. Perhaps Millicent was permitted on this occasion to work this rather special bowl on her own and was then allowed to have it marked in Arundel Street in Sheffield by a maker she had previously known. The School of Art had been in Arundel Street near William Gallimore's workshop. Possibly she had worked for them before she went to London.

The two men were defining a new generation of craftsmen, adhering to the guiding tenets of quality of design and craftsmanship. They were also making friendships and forging collaborations which would continue throughout their working lives. They were active in professional associations such as the Art Workers' Guild, the Arts and Crafts Exhibition Society, the Church Crafts League and the Design and Industries Association. They aspired to move forward from the Victorian age and were ready to embrace the new century.

1 *Sheffield School of Art Reports 1881–1901*, Adsetts Special Collection, Sheffield Hallam University

2 *A School of Art is Beginning, part 1 1843–1963*, Dr John Basford, 2013, Sheffield Hallam University.

3 *Sheffield and Rotherham Independent*, 27 September 1888, p7, column 2.

4 Ibid. 24 November 1896, p4, column 8

5 *School of Art Report*, 1893

6 Ibid 1896.

7 *The Artist*, 1902, p115–118

8 'Model of a Ceremonial Key', *Mapping the Practice and Profession of Sculpture in Britain and Ireland 1851–1951*, University of Glasgow History of Art and HATII, online database 2011 [http://sculpture.gla.ac.uk/view/object.php?id=msib5_1208290506, accessed 01 Dec 2016]

9 Catalogue of the Spring Exhibition, The City Art Gallery, Leeds, 1897, p78, 827,828. p82, 867

10 *The Studio, The National Competition:* South Kensington, J. W. Gleeson- White, Vol.8, no. 42, September 1896, pp224–237. Copy PHA.

CHAPTER 4

The Earliest Years in London

Having spent about nine years together in friendship, study and rivalry, once they had completed the academic year ending summer 1897, the pair spent several months travelling through the cities of Europe, supported by scholarships. Accounts of which places they visited vary, the account in the *Sheffield Weekly News* of October 1899 says that they:

> ... put into practice a long contemplated project: a Continental tour. Although the object of their tour was Italy, the Mecca of all artists, they visited Paris, the home of technique. The long famous metalwork of Southern Germany also attracted their attention. Through Switzerland to Italy ... in the byways of Lombardy and the uplands of Tuscany ... The majority of their time, of course, was spent in Florence, Venice and Naples, with its magnificent collection of bronzes, and the beautiful articles of common use made by the Greek artists during the Roman Empire, and so carefully preserved for us under the soft ashes of Vesuvius.[1]

In an article Ramsden wrote thirty years later he said:

> I was brought up on classic details, and when about to proceed abroad on a travelling scholarship was actually forbidden to open a sketch book until Italy was reached. I remember pleading that as we had to pass through Rouen, I would like to stay there a day or two to view its Cathedral but I was told that there was nothing for a designer to study in France except the Italian things in the Museums of Paris, and it was better to proceed straight to the fountainhead of art.[2]

He does not say from whom this advice came, but it seems that they were given credentials through the Director of Art, a Mr Thomas Armstrong, which brought them the help of Italian government officials and museum curators which must have been enormously useful to them. They had the opportunity to look, to study, to sketch and to photograph. The small folio/sketchbook in the Decorative Arts Department of Museums Sheffield is a rare souvenir of Ramsden's sketches of the period. His name and Sheffield address are handwritten on the inside cover, and as he left home for good about 1897/8, it is reasonable to assume the sketches pre-date this time. They are on loose-leaf pages in pencil and watercolour and include architectural details and objects. One of them is a chalice, sketched in pencil and watercolour, perhaps one he had seen on his European travels. Several architectural details have a handwritten note indicating they were made in Venice.

Sketches from Ramsden's early notebook, about 1897. (*Author's photos*)

Enriched and inspired by their experiences, on their return the young men set up together in London. By now they were twenty-five and twenty-six and had many years of practical experience behind them. Omar had the usual artisan board school education, was apprenticed at fourteen and had been working, studying and teaching since then. Alwyn had been working from at least the age of eighteen and studying for ten years. They had to study part-time at the end of a day's work, before winning the scholarships which allowed full-time study. Every achievement had come from their own dedication. Both had excellent records as students and must have felt excited and confident enough start up on their own.

They have frequently been referred to as 'Arts and Crafts silversmiths'. But although many of their works, particularly the earliest ones, had many characteristics of the Arts and Crafts 'style', neither man held the socio-political views central to the ideas of Ruskin, Morris or Ashbee. These men came from much more privileged backgrounds than Ramsden and Carr, they had the support of prosperous parents, public school and university education and upper middle-class connections. Ramsden and Carr had to work their own way up in the world. Importantly, though, they shared the Arts and Crafts passion for hand-crafted work versus mass production, for quality of materials, for individuality of design and a love of art.

Their first working premises were in the Stamford Bridge Studios, 16 Wandon Road, off the Fulham Road and opposite Chelsea station. Home to several artists and craftspeople, the studios were primitive even then and were later pulled down and replaced by purpose-built studios.

These were humble premises for the two at the start of their London careers, though their hopes and ambitions were anything but humble. Once back from their European travels, in February 1898 they registered their own joint mark at the London Assay Office from this address and must have been thrilled to do so.[3] Their first task was to fulfil the important commission for the Sheffield mace which Omar had won in competition and they worked together to make it. Alwyn's brother Arthur tells a story which illustrates the modest conditions of their workplace:

> These were their Bohemian days: locks and bolts on doors were far from secure and it not infrequently happened that the two young collaborators paid their evening visits or stood in theatre queues with their overcoat pockets bulging with the precious but unfinished portions of the repoussé masterpiece in silver they were engaged upon at the moment.[4]

Despite these difficulties the mace was eventually completed but not before they had months of problems. It seemed desirable for it to bear the hallmark of its own city of Sheffield, and a letter from Mr B Watson, the Sheffield Assay Master advised them that 'As your mark is not registered here it will be necessary to get this done'. He asked for the mace to be sent to him to obtain a sample for the assay. This letter was sent in December 1898, and their own mark registered in Sheffield in January 1899, but it was not until 15 June 1899 that Mr Watson received Omar's letter explaining that I have 'strengthened it [the mace] with extra silver and in so doing have obliterated the assay mark'. The Assay Master was very disapproving, telling Omar that he had thus 'committed the offence (Penalty £10) of adding silver to a Hallmarked article … the proper course is to obtain consent of the hall *before such alteration or addition is made*'. Further, 'it is an offence to fraudulently obliterate a Hallmark from any ware'. Had Ramsden complied with the right procedures only the additions of silver would have had to be tested, whereas now, 'the whole of the top will have to be scraped'. Given his regrettable behaviour, Ramsden was not allowed any credit and had to send a halfpenny per ounce of silver in advance to pay for the cost.

The letter of reply from the Assay Master on the 19 June admonished him yet more severely, while it did acknowledge receipt of Ramsden's five shilling Postal Order:

> We regret you have not complied with our request for the exhibition

of the whole of the mace and we must insist upon this being done...
You do not appear to know that it is an offence for which there is a
heavy penalty to pull a ware to pieces and alter it in any way after it
has left the Hall. Awaiting receipt of the mace.

On 23 June the last letter was sent to Ramsden and Carr: 'The parcel
and postcard came to hand this morning. The lid has been re-assayed
and the whole despatched this evening per registered Parcel Post'.
Ramsden had obviously complained about a delay, which seems
unrepentant considering that his errors had protracted the whole
affair: 'We regret the delay arising from the insufficient address on
our letter of the 19th but without the envelope we cannot trace the
offender'.[5]

Ramsden's or Carr's replies are not recorded or kept, letters to
them were addressed to both. When the mace was finally presented
in the city in October that year everyone appeared to be very pleased
with it. This rather acrimonious correspondence is in the Sheffield
archives; perhaps it continued to irritate Ramsden as he later made
several critical remarks suggesting that the hallmarking system was
over-officious. However, the pair had learned a valuable lesson at
an early stage. As they became more renowned and won significant
public and private commissions, their awareness of the need for good
administration would have proved invaluable.

In 1893 Sheffield had been granted 'The Style and Charter of City'
by Her Majesty Queen Victoria, and the building of an appropriately
fine town hall, still there, had begun in 1891. It seems that no expense
was spared in the fitting out; fine local marbles adorn the entrance walls
and staircase, there is handsome oak panelling and carving in the wide
corridors and there was electric lighting throughout. The building cost
£175,737 14s 10d including the site, a fitting hall for a wealthy city.[6]

The project was an opportunity for local artisans to show the skills of
design and craftsmanship which the art school had been established to
encourage. Queen Victoria opened the building in 1897 and the Duke
of Norfolk, a major local landowner and MP became the first Lord

Mayor. He was to be Omar's first patron. As noted, the Duke had set up a competition for the design of a ceremonial mace for the city which Omar had won, with a substantial money prize. The Duke also defrayed the cost of its construction, which must have been considerable. In this context the selection of the design of a young local student rather than an established firm was a distinct achievement for both Omar and for the school.

A mace is part of the traditional regalia of a city or institution and its presentation was an important local event. It took place with all due ceremony in October 1899, to general acclamation, and with wide and detailed local press coverage. The *Sheffield Daily Telegraph*, The *Weekly News*, and The *Sheffield and Rotherham Independent* gave full and illustrated accounts of the mace, the presentation ceremony and the local makers: [7]

> A mace represents the Royal Authority invested in the mayor and is carried before him in all public ceremonies. The earliest maces, as borne by the royal sergeants-at-arms, were actually weapons.

The offensive role gradually dwindled and royal authority became symbolised by placing the royal arms at the ends of the mace.

The Duke was intent on incorporating the correct symbolism, both for the city and for his own family. In his presentation speech he said:

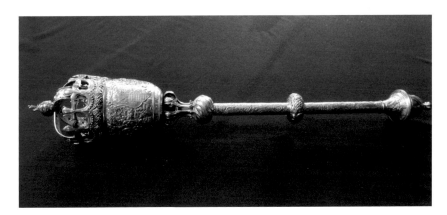

The Sheffield Mace, 2015. (*Author's photo*)

In presenting the mace, I felt it should be not only a work of art, but should have connected with it all those historical and antiquarian associations which are generally considered to be represented by those ancient symbols of authority, and I therefore had recourse to my friend, Mr St John Hope, a very distinguished antiquarian ... I am sure that all those connected with himself in the production of this mace owe him great gratitude ... for the valuable antiquarian knowledge he placed at the service of those who designed the mace.

This suggests a considerable degree of cooperation between the Duke, Mr St John Hope and the young designer in working out the precise detail of the symbolism of the decoration. It was not left to Ramsden to decide on the detail. The 1973 catalogue states disparagingly that he won the competition with a finished design which displayed 'beefy historicism'. Surely any 'beefy historicism' was the result of Ramsden carrying out the very specific wishes of his patron?

The *Weekly News* on October 14 (from a press cutting in Paul Hallam's archive) reported that:

The design of the mace has been founded on traditional lines of the best maces of the 16th and 17th centuries, while the ornament applied has a distinct symbolical or historical meaning to the city to which it is to belong...On one side of the head are the arms of Sheffield, on the other those of the Duke of Norfolk, the donor. Midway between these are two York roses. The intervening space is entirely covered with oak leaves and acorns, the badge of the Duke of Norfolk. Between two brightly burnished mouldings on the base runs the motto of the city, *Deo Adjuvante Labor Proficit*. [With God's Help, Our Labour is Successful.] And underneath is the quaint inscription, 'Omar Ramsden and Alwyn C. E. Carr made me in the year of our Lord 1899.

The arms of Sheffield show sheaths of corn, perhaps a play on the city's name, which derives from the River Sheath, the Sheath-field. The staff is decorated with pomegranates, emblem of Mary Tudor's mother Catherine of Aragon, Queen Mary having granted Sheffield its first charter. The whole was heavily water-gilt. The article continued:

> … bringing out the exquisite modelling displayed throughout the work. Although there is nothing weirdly new or eccentric in this design it is thoroughly good in style, character and workmanship, and suitable for the work it is destined to fulfil and will rank according to experts among the finest maces in Europe … an additional interest is lent to the mace by the fact that it is the work of two young artist craftsmen, natives and educated in Sheffield and in consequence the mace bears the Sheffield assay mark.

Accepting the mace on behalf of the Sheffield Corporation, the Lord Mayor said that 'it was especially gratifying to know that the mace was the work of two Sheffielders – (hear, hear) – and that their names would be handed down to posterity by it'.

It was an excellent start to the business partnership and would have given them first rate references and useful connections for future commissions. Mr St John Hope is thought to have been influential in stimulating Ramsden's interest in historic silver, including the mazers he was later to develop, and he introduced Ramsden to Mr William Watts, First Keeper of Metalwork at the Victoria & Albert Museum.

Once the mace was satisfactorily completed, the pair worked together at building up a business, looking for commissions and exhibiting where they could. From the beginning, most of their work had the visibly hammered finish characteristic of Arts and Crafts pieces. This gave evidence of their having been made by hand; machine-made silver was customarily polished to smoothness. Enamels and semi-precious stones were selected for decoration rather than the high-value precious stones considered showy. The mediaeval period was referenced in decoration, calligraphy and the quotation of such verse as Tennyson's 'Lady of Shalott'. Quotations relating to rural English life, as in Spenser's 'Shephearde's Calendar', were admired, as were naturalistic motifs of flowers and foliage, or influences of Celtic design.

Just a few of their other earliest works have a nineteenth century hallmark. Ian Pickford relates an anecdote in his article on Ramsden in *Antique Collecting* magazine:

> Some years ago, at one of my lectures, a lady produced a most fascinating early piece – a hand mirror struck with the date for 1897/8. The story behind it gives a wonderful insight into how Ramsden and Carr initially established themselves. The lady related to me how her grandfather had had an important business in Bond Street and that one day a young man entered saying that he was newly qualified and was trying, with his partner, to establish a business. Her grandfather was impressed with his enterprise and commissioned the mirror as a present (the first of several) for his wife. The young man was, of course, Omar Ramsden. This mirror, with its 1897/8 hallmark could only have been made within a period of about twelve weeks and may be their very first piece! So far, I have not come across any other with this date letter.[8]

A design for a hand mirror brought one of Omar's early prizes from art school, he probably adapted successful designs for later inspiration. Every lady at that time would hope to have a set of silver brushes, mirror and ivory comb for her dressing table.

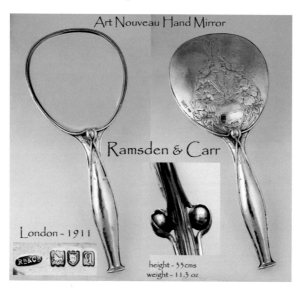

Silver Hand Mirror, 1911. (*Courtesy of Silverman Antiques*)

Still in the nineteenth century, soon after registering their mark, Ramsden and Carr made a series of plaques for Oxford Colleges, on behalf of Payne and Son, long established silversmiths and jewellers of Oxford. Paynes had opened in Wallingford about 1790 and has had premises at 131 High Street, Oxford since 1888. It is still run by the seventh generation of the family, Judy Payne, with an eighth member learning the business. The firm of James Rogers and Sons, craftsmen in wood, was further along the High Street at number fifty-one. Rogers made stands for Ramsden's work, and turned his mazer bowls. They traded there for nearly fifty years but closed in 1952, the premises are now a tea room.

Geoffrey Payne, Judy's Great-uncle, was a particularly talented artist-craftsman who went to work in Ramsden and Carr's Maxwell Road workshop in 1901 when he was sixteen. His mother's diary relates how she took him to Fulham and settled him into lodgings with a Mrs Bygott in Perrymead Street, ten minutes from the workshop, he started working for them at 8am on Saturday morning. Geoffrey moved on to the Birmingham Municipal School of Art then opened a workshop of his own in Oxford in 1907. The next year he took up a position as instructor at the Keswick School of Industrial Art, renowned as a centre for Arts and Craft work under Canon Rawnsley. Unhappily his promising career ended when he died after an operation for appendicitis in October, he was only twenty-three.

Another nineteenth century work in the Museums Sheffield collection is a deep bowl decorated with wild roses and briars, dated 1899. The repoussé calligraphy is in a font which suggests the mediaeval, of the kind William Morris had created – the Golden and the Troy – for his Kelmscott Press. The quotation is from *The Shepheardes Calendar, September*, by sixteenth century English poet, Edmund Spenser, 'Content who lives with tried state, need fear no change of frowning fate.' Quotations are characteristic of Arts and Crafts work, Ramsden and Carr frequently used them. In *Who's Who* of 1936 Alwyn Carr listed 'poetic drama' as one of his interests. The rather long inscription inside states 'Omar Ramsden and Alwyn C. E. Carr made me in the year 1899.' Carr owned this bowl himself for some years; after his death in 1940 his residuary legatees presented it to Sheffield Museum in his memory. Again, this may suggest that he was primarily responsible for its design and perhaps the making.

Silver bowl with a quotation from 'The Shephearde's Calender' by Edmund Spenser, 1899. (*Sheffield Galleries and Museums Trust*)

Also dated 1899 is a vase, two very similar ones are dated 1900 and 1901. The first is about 28cm high, decorated with pomegranates and a Greek inscription translated as 'Beloved Co-worker', presumably made by one of the partners for the other, I would think given by Alwyn to Omar.

The second is similarly decorated, but without a personal inscription and on an octagonal marble stand; it was acquired by the Victoria and Albert Museum in 1900 for fifteen guineas. For silversmiths so early in their careers, it must have been very gratifying to have this important

museum buying their work, at quite considerable cost. The third is a
similar size and shape but the repoussé decoration is floral rather than of
fruit; it was formerly in the Campbell Collection. All three show distinct
Art Nouveau influence in their rhythmical elegance of line and their
stylisation of natural motifs. All have the inscription under the foot,
'Omar Ramsden & Alwyn C. E. Carr made me', as yet still in English.

As more commissions came their way they could afford to move
from Stamford Bridge to better premises, and by 1901, as young men
of twenty-seven and twenty-eight they found accommodation at Albert
Studios, south of the Albert Bridge and opposite Battersea Park. It was
a row of eight very small but decorative and charming houses purpose
built as studios at the rear of the much larger and grander Albert
Mansions, (now Albany Mansions) in Albert Bridge Road, Battersea.

The Albert Studios today, 2016. (*Author's photo*)

They had been designed in 1894 and built for a J. P. Kennedy who lived at 10 Albert Mansions. Perhaps he had a personal interest in encouraging artists and craftsmen. Omar and Alwyn lived there until about 1904. Quite possibly they heard about the studios from their art school friend from Sheffield, Edward Wigfull, who lived in another of the studio cottages with his older brother. Other craftsmen and women living there included a textile designer, painters, sculptors, a book illustrator, a stained glass maker and a furniture designer; several became successful and well known in their fields. At one end of the row lived Percy William Gibbs, a gifted painter of landscapes and pretty women in fashionable Edwardian dress, and later in the post-war fashions of the 1920s. Born in the East End of London where his father was an upholsterer, like Ramsden and Carr he had benefited from the government's well established training in art schools. After his time at the Albert Studios his success enabled him to move to the very desirable River Bank in Kingston, looking over the Thames towards Hampton Court Palace. George Morrow and his brother Edwin lived at the other end of the row at number one, two of the eight sons of a painter and decorator from Belfast, of whom four became artists. George achieved fame as a book illustrator and cartoonist, joining the influential magazine *Punch* in 1924, where he stayed for over twenty-five years, becoming Art Editor. He illustrated the popular books of E. V. Lucas, another member of the Punch staff who deserved recognition for introducing his *Punch* colleague A. A. Milne to illustrator Ernest Shepard, resulting in the celebrated collaboration over Winnie the Pooh. This was a hotbed of creative activity where artistic talent could flourish.

Even in these early days at Albert Studios, Carr and Ramsden's work was attracting favourable attention. *The Artist* published a review of their metalwork in 1902 which is particularly interesting as it includes their less well known domestic works in several different metals: handsome door fittings, a wrought iron fire basket, a shield and a design for a hanging lamp bearing Carr's signature.

Left: Lamp signed by Carr, illustrated in 'The Artist', 1902. (*Out of copyright*)

It has already been noted that as students both had designed decorative yet functional domestic fittings; Alwyn had a prize for his scheme for the back of a dog stove, Omar for a design for an electric light pendant. The illustrations show different versions of their distinguishing sign of hammer and wings; at the top of a doorplate, on a cigarette case and on the fire basket.

The winged hammer motif, used by the partnership and by both men separately, 1902. (*Out of copyright*)

The rather wordy reviewer, 'JSR', seemed to be a practical man, he was not quite so keen on the wings and hammer in the fire basket:

> The design of wings in the back panel appears rather busy for the rest of the work; it would, of course, soon be obscured by smoke, and the cavities filled with soot, but – reverting to one's utilitarian views – is it advisable to provide lodgement for such undesirable acquaintances? We must not neglect the housewife's claims.

A shield was found 'eminently satisfactory', though 'one could have wished the tips of the lions tails ... bore less resemblance to tulips; but, after all, it is fun, easy and safe to poke fun at an heraldic lion.'

J. S. R. discussed contemporary interest in the 'somewhat rude' aspects of mediaeval metalwork, particularly in relation to the 'beautiful door furnishings, (affixed evidently merely for the purpose of showing their quality...)' He considered that they showed 'how quaint beauty of design may be yet thoroughly adaptable to modern architecture...'[9] The door has fine examples of Arts and Crafts fittings, hinges, fingerplates and handle. I wonder what house it is gracing today?

An article in *The Studio* the next year also admired a house where Ramsden and Carr's 'enamelled finger plates relieve the oak doors with a fine touch of colour'. It had been claimed as early as 1899 that:

> They have already fitted up with special metalwork the houses which several London architects have recently built for themselves ... each object so produced has a charm and individuality which alone can satisfy the growing art feeling of the educated classes of modern times.[10]

Another early twentieth century work was a fine silver rose bowl, inscribed 'Flowers are the playthings fair left by angels long ago'. Underneath is inscribed 'Ramsden and Carr Made Me In the Year 1902, London SW'), proving that the pair were equally competent at producing more decorative pieces as well as practical ones.

In December 1902 they held an exhibition at 12 Old Burlington

Street; it was to be a couple more years before they were to have their own exhibiting studio. A selection of maces and chains was displayed, including the Sheffield and University of London maces; 'owing to the fact that hand processes alone have been used in its execution the University of London mace shown has much of the individuality of old work'. The mayoral chain and badge of Woolwich in hand beaten gold and enamels were displayed also. The exhibition was well reviewed and illustrated in January by *The House, Journal of Home Arts and Crafts*.[11]

The Builder, of 28 November 1903, mentioned a small Arts and Crafts exhibition at the Woodbury Gallery, where C. R. Ashbee often displayed work. 'A set of silver salt, pepper and mustard pots, exhibited by Messrs Ramsden, Omar and A. C. E. Carr have a good solid character'.

In 1904, *The Studio: an illustrated magazine of fine and applied art*, edited by J. W. Gleeson-White, who had commented favourably on a work of Ramsden's in his student days, published reviews of the partnership's work in vol. 30 and vol. 32 as well as a particularly full and wide-ranging appreciation of Ramsden and Carr's work, by Esther Wood. She wrote:

> It was once said of Rossetti that there was more 'fundamental brain-work' in his art than in that of all the other Pre-Raphaelites put together. The phrase recurs in looking at the wonderfully versatile and eclectic work of Messrs Ramsden and Carr – on the one hand, so scholarly, so literary … but so workmanlike, so scrupulously adapted to practical needs.

She recognised:

> the finest detail as well as in the general method and habit of the fingers, and then adding whatever the modern world might yield of apt invention and inspiration for practical things … few had put so much historical research and historical knowledge into the building up of their designs … [they displayed] an intellectual bias with original creative power, a fine discrimination in the use of material, and an imaginative and poetic sense of decoration.

Mention was made of their device:

> For their own 'craft-mark' these designers have adopted the striking figure of a winged hammer, which is very successfully used in the back of the fire grate in their own studio – a massive and dignified piece of workmanship bespeaking homely comfort with its big standards and supports for fire-irons, its roomy hood and chimney, and its ample spaces for keeping omelettes and muffins laudably hot. The simplicity and appropriateness of the 'winged hammer' device enables it to be repeated in many forms – even in a book-plate and stationery.[12]

Both men continued to use versions of the winged hammer after they dissolved their partnership. Carr also requested in his will that his grave stone be marked with the device.

Attention from the press continued: *The Art Journal* described an exhibition at the Woodbury Gallery: 'Prominent in the number of exhibits and place assigned to it was the repoussé and handbeaten silver work of Mr Omar Ramsden and Mr Alwyn C. E. Carr. These workers, though well enough known to those who may be called the private public, are not known through their exhibitions, except, perhaps, by the duplicate of the lily vase which was bought for the national collection at South Kensington'. Also mentioned was the Omar Khayam wine cup and the 'Masks' cup.

The young pair's fame and reputation was spreading and by 1905 their work was beginning to be featured in European publications too. In August, there was a detailed article in *Kunst und Kunsthandwerk* – translated Arts and Crafts – published in Vienna by the prestigious Verlag von Artaria & Co.[13] The cover is elegantly illustrated, with a decorative Art Nouveau edging.

The photographs include examples of Ramsden and Carr's works in different metals; a trowel with an ivory handle decorated with enamel (incidentally spelled e-mail in German) made to celebrate the laying of the foundation stone of the Court of Appeal in London. The bronze hanging lamp shown in *The Artist* review of 1902 is illustrated, and a

Front cover of Viennese 'Kunst und Kunsthandwerk', 1905. (*Out of copyright*)

silvered bronze doorplate and handle, plus several silver pieces in the Arts and Crafts style characteristic of their early partnership years.

One of their earliest commemorative cups was illustrated. The edge has a rich band of decoration set with enamels and emblematic shields. This commission uses the terminology of the time, it was made for 'The Staff of Native Chiefs', Lahore. The original *Punjab Chiefs College* was renamed Aitchison College in 1886 in honour of Sir Charles

Umpherston Aitchison, Lieutenant Governor of the Punjab. He had encouraged its foundation on the lines of British public schools for the sons of the most important chiefs, nobles and rulers. It remains a prestigious educational establishment, now in Pakistan.

The Studio and *The Artist* continued to review the partnership's work very favourably for a number of years, as did *The Art Journal,* which in 1907 included a photograph in one of its articles of the 'State Entrance Gates to the Newgate Sessions House, Old Bailey, designed and wrought in iron and bronze' which was one of the heaviest works they undertook. The following year *The Journal* featured an article on 'Fine Church Metalwork' and included photographs of Ramsden and Carr's Westminster Cathedral monstrance as well as their 'great gates for the New Bailey'. It appears that the partnership could produce great works, on a large scale, for both the sacred and the secular worlds.

In contrast, they also produced much smaller and more intimate and personal pieces in the form of jewellery. A silver, amethyst and enamel pendant, with a handmade silver chain, dated 1905, is an example very much in the Arts and Crafts style, depicting a mermaid looking into a mirror. The enamel work was probably done by Carr; he is known to have done some enamel work around this time, probably including the Westminster Cathedral monstrance. The necklace was once part of the extensive collection of the late Mrs Hull Grundy, who donated this and several Ramsden and Carr pieces to the Wilson Gallery, Cheltenham and several other museums. Mrs Hull Grundy would receive curators while sitting in her bed, interviewing them to see whether she considered them suitable recipients for pieces from her vast collection.

Museums Sheffield has some beautifully handcrafted teaspoons of this early period, all different but all showing the hammer marks on the bowls so distinctive of Arts and Crafts work. They were formerly part of the significant Bill Brown Cutlery Collection.

When not working on special orders for commissions, the craftsmen would be usefully employed making articles for stock, including a wide

Three decorative teaspoons from the Bill Brown Collection, Sheffield, 1910, 1904 and 1912. (*Sheffield Galleries and Museums Trust*)

variety of domestic articles were made for use in the home. Though very occasionally of lesser quality and lighter weight, they were usually beautiful pieces in their own right, perhaps a tea or coffee pot, hot water jug, sugar box and tongs, and milk or cream jug, on a matching silver tray. Vases, cigarette boxes and cases, dishes for sweetmeats, dressing table sets, all were popular. Biscuit boxes, inkwells and desk sets, candlesticks, condiment sets, decorative boxes, goblets, crumb scoops, sugar sifters, fruit bowls, rose bowls, cake stands, jewellery caskets, christening cups, claret jugs; the list is long, as both men worked steadily for nearly forty years. There were also works in heavier metals, like the door furniture, light fittings and fire irons reviewed in The Artist of 1902, and the gates made for the Old Bailey and the Stanmore hospital.

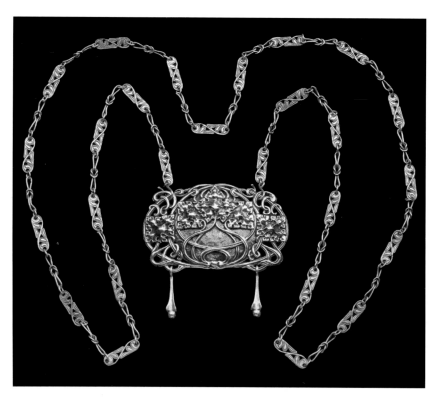

Above and opposite: Silver and enamel pendants and a buckle.
(*Courtesy of Van den Bosch*)

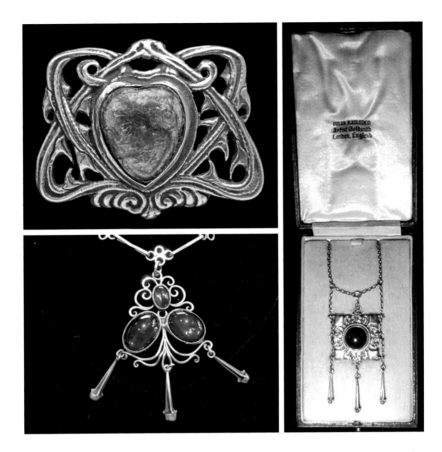

Given the pair's ability to design and execute an enormous variety of pieces, and with such skill and artistry, it is little surprise that, in 1903 Ramsden was invited into membership of the prestigious Art Workers Guild. Alwyn was elected the following year. Membership was by invitation only, and required submission of work to a committee of existing members for their approval. Both partners were accepted relatively early in their careers. In *The Art Workers Guild, 125 Years*, Alan Powers describes the criteria for election today, which sounds like that in Ramsden and Carr's time:

> The nature of the Guild's elective system means that members are proposed and elected on grounds that are not primarily about style … when the work of aspirant members is shown to the committee … a number of criteria are used in making decisions…. the sense of

personal commitment in the form of training and career, involving skill and the creation of a body of work ... working to commission ... and collaboration with other artists and designers ... the idea of artistic service instead of artistic ego...[14]

The Guild had been formed in 1884 by several artists at the heart of what was to become the Arts and Crafts movement. It was partly in response to the perceived snobbery of the Royal Academy, which was unwilling to recognise artist craftsmen as being of sufficient intellectual standing to permit them to membership. The Royal Academy recognised only painters, sculptors, architects and engravers and not the new arts of design. Early Guild members included C. R. Ashbee, William Morris, Walter Crane, W. R. Lethaby and several other architects. Crane had been Master of the Guild from 1888–1889; a few years later he was presenting student awards to Omar, Alwyn and others in Sheffield.

Guild members had established the Arts and Crafts Exhibition Society in 1888, as a separate forum for displaying and selling their work; this was the first use of the phrase 'Arts and Crafts'. Later, from 1929 to 1937 Ramsden was President of the society. Within the Guild likeminded artists/craftsmen could meet, hear lectures, (including several by Ramsden), talk about artistic issues of the day and mix socially. It strongly affirmed that members were not mere artisans carrying out their patrons' orders, but creative artists of professional standing. This argument regarding status went back at least as far as sixteenth century Italy. Master Goldsmith Benvenuto Cellini had argued passionately for equality of status between the fine and decorative arts. C. R. Ashbee must have considered Cellini's ideas as relevant to the discussions of the day as he translated many of his writings into English. Cellini was the goldsmith with whom Ramsden was compared by some in an enthusiastic obituary after his death, although Ramsden had very critical words to say about Cellini's ability as a silver designer on more than one occasion.

A qualification for membership of the Guild was to show the intellectual capacity for design in addition to craftsmanship in making;

making to another's design, however skilled, was not sufficient. Powers notes that many of the early distinguished and influential architects, including Lethaby, Edwin Lutyens, and Norman Jewson, necessarily cooperated closely with artist craftsmen of all kinds in the completion of their commissions, including stained glass designers, furniture makers, wood carvers, tile makers and metalworkers, many of the most creative men of the time. Ramsden and Carr's contemporaries there included Ashbee, as architect, silversmith, furniture designer; Ernest Gimson and Sidney and Ernest Barnsley, the arts and crafts designers from the Cotswolds; Roger Fry, the influential art critic; painter Augustus John; and Christopher Whall, designer of Arts and Crafts stained glass. George Bernard Shaw was an honorary member. Eric Gill was elected a member in the same year as Alwyn, as a letter cutter and sign writer. In his autobiography in 1909 Gill wrote what might be a description of the ideology of the Guild, 'I was reuniting what should never have been separated: the artist as man of imagination and the artist as workman'.[15]

When Alwyn Carr made his will in 1938 he left detailed instructions for the design of his grave and memorial stone, including a wish that it be designed by Laurence Turner, who had previously made William Morris's simple grave in Kelmscott.

Amongst other skills, Turner was a specialist in the field of decorative plasterwork characteristic of Arts and Crafts buildings, working with many progressive architects. He was not only a designer, but was happy to work at the messy business of plasterwork in his workshop, where he employed several craftsmen. He was an active member of the Art Workers Guild for over sixty years and Master in 1922, taking part in their exhibitions and giving dozens of talks there.[16] One of Turner's best known works is the 'New Shop' for Liberty's in Argyll Place off Regent Street. He cut the half timbers which ornament the building from the one-hundred year-old 'Hindustan'. A *Spectator* article of 20 August 1976 suggested that this half-timbered effect was later copied in the gables of thousands of 'Mock-Tudor' semis in the 1930s.

If Turner was unable for any reason to design his grave, Carr requested that only another fellow member was to be given the commission. He left money for this and a further bequest of £100 to the Guild. The finished gravestone was well done; Alwyn would surely have been pleased with the result.

The Guild was important to its members as a support and social meeting place; as Powers says, it performed something of the function of a Gentlemens' Club. Annual outings were arranged for members; photographs of two of the outings are included in Powers' book. The members – all male of course until 1966 – look very cheerful and sociable. Amateur dramatics were a regular part of the proceedings, one imagines that Ramsden and Carr would have taken an active role in the productions as, by repute, they were great lovers of drama and amateur theatricals.

Later members included Sir Basil Spence, Ronald Searle, Rex Whistler, Kenneth Clark, Leslie Durbin, and John Betjeman. Contemporary members are illustrated in the 125-year anniversary book with brief résumés of their work to date; they show a hugely diverse range of skills at a high level, from lute-making to embroidery, from museum designer to stoneworker. Being elected to membership at such an early stage in Ramsden and Carr's career together shows both their dedication and professionalism and would no doubt have helped to plot their course for greater things yet to come.

---

1 *Weekly News*, Sheffield, 14 October 1899.

2 *Goldsmiths Journal*, 1929 p909

3 London Assay Office, February 1898

4 Arthur Carr, notes, 1940.

5 *Sheffield Assay Office, Letter Book 7*, 1877–79, p363, 14 December 1898 and *Letter Book 8* 1899, 15 June p72/3, June 19 p77, June 23 p82. Letters to Ramsden and Carr, Sheffield Archives.

6 *Description of Sheffield Town Hall, Illustrated*, Alfred Fletcher, 1897. Sheffield Local Studies Library.

7 *Sheffield Daily Telegraph*, 10 October 1899 and *Sheffield and Rotherham Independent*, 11 October 1899

8 *Antique Collecting*, November 2003, Volume 38, no. 6, Ian Pickford.

9 *The Artist, Metal Work by Ramsden and Carr*, JSR, 1902, pp115–118, Copy in Adsetts Special Collection, Sheffield Hallam University.

10 *Weekly News*, Sheffield, October 14th 1899.

11 *The House, Journal of Home Arts and Crafts*, January 1903.

12 *The Studio*, 1904, vol 32, pp21-26, Some Metal-Work by Omar Ramsden and Alwyn C. E. Carr. Esther Wood. Copy in Adsetts.

13 *Metallarbeiten von Omar Ramsden und Alwyn Carr, P.G.Konody, in Kunst und Kunsthandwerk,* 1905, vol 8 pp 167–174. Trans. Paula Lee, University of Chicago. Copy PHA.

14 The *Art Workers Guild*, 125 Years, Lara Platman, Unicorn Press, 2009, text by Alan Powers.

15 *Autobiography*, Eric Gill, London, 1940, Jonathon Cape, p162.

16 Laurence Arthur Turner, *Mapping the Practice and Profession of Sculpture in Britain and Ireland 1851–1951*, University of Glasgow History of Art and HATII, online database 2011.

CHAPTER 5

Life at St Dunstan's Studio

The first years in partnership were successful, financially as well as critically, and the pair could now afford to move to much larger premises. In 1904 they submitted plans for a combined home and exhibiting studio in South Kensington, the original planning application is still in the Kensington and Chelsea Archives.[1]

The chosen site in Seymour Place, now Seymour Walk, was reputed to be on Nell Gwynn's former mulberry garden, only ten minutes' walk along the Fulham Road to the workshop at the rear of 38 Maxwell Road. Some of the craftsmen, including Leslie Durbin, thought that Ramsden owned number 38 and let it to someone the craftsmen never met. Apparently Omar would often cycle there, usually accompanied by one of the terriers they always kept, possibly the one called Michael, or Michael II, who sat in his office.

Ramsden and Carr must have moved into the site as soon as possible, as records show details of Christmas selling exhibitions here from the end of 1903. They were to become an annual event, always advertised in *The Times*. The *Sheffield Daily Telegraph* reviewed the first exhibition very favourably on 5 December 1903 as part of their regular London *Correspondence by Private Wire*.[2] The writer had appraised their work in the preceding spring and was charmed to find that this exhibition was even better. He acknowledged their sound technical background of silversmithing, as well as their 'rare and notable qualities of design and craftsmanship'. He considered that:

> In an exhibition of what has come to be somewhat vaguely termed 'arts and craft work' one is not prepared to find, in the first place,

craftsmanship, nor, in the second place, art which expressed more than eccentricity, but the craft of Mr Ramsden and Mr Carr is founded on a wholesome apprenticeship to smith work.

From this same review came the information that the Victoria & Albert Museum had acquired an electrotype replica of the Sheffield mace, particularly noted as it was the only mace in the museum collection which was of a later date than the Queen Anne period.

One week later, as part of the report on the achievements of their Technical School of Art, the same Sheffield paper gave a fuller review of the exhibits at the St Dunstan's studio – '*Former Students' London Exhibition*', 'Mr Ramsden was one of the first batch of free students, and received his early education at Crookes Church School'. Assuming this is correct, it reveals where Omar went to school as a child before and after the family went to the United States. The writer particularly admired the set of twelve spoons similar to traditional Apostle spoons but with finials 'representing Saints of the Early English Calendar including St Chad, Dunstan, Aidan, Cuthbert and others. The figures are exquisitely worked, minutely and yet so as to endure and still to be practical for use'.

The reviewer did, however, see 'a certain tinge of conservatism in ornament' but found that appropriate. He also noted with pleasure the several seals made 'by these two exponents of art metal work [which] make it quite evident that they possess the ability for an important revival … those for the Bishops of Worcester and Exeter especially call for commendation'. He admired the 'bowls, enamelled chains and pendants, and works of various descriptions in iron and brass'. He judged that given their artistic merit 'the articles are on sale at exceedingly moderate prices'.

No doubt the pair were buoyed by their successes and threw themselves wholeheartedly into the project of designing and building. They chose Charles H. B. Quennell as their architect and builder William Willett carried out the construction. Willett is a man much better known for his inventive ideas for advancing and putting back the clock according to the season, to increase daylight hours. As Ramsden and Carr had such firm ideas about design, they would have given a great deal of thought to their choice of architect, and would have collaborated closely with whomever they appointed. Charles Quennell had won the National Gold Medal for Architectural Design in South Kensington in 1895 and had a particular interest in relating garden design and furnishings to a house.

According to his son Peter, Charles Quennell:

> ...had much to recommend him. His morals were sound; he was a notably hard worker; and he had already established a reputation among rising English architects...a staunch supporter of the post-Ruskinian Arts and Crafts movement [he] not only planned buildings but had designed a variety of domestic objects … chairs, tables, bookcases, bedsteads and simple but handsome garden-seats, made of solid English oak instead of Victorian cast iron.[3]

Early photographs show Carr and Ramsden (together with the Downs Butcher family who were to live at St Dunstan's later) having tea on just that kind of curved oak garden seating known from Quennell's

Ramsden, with Anne and Charles Downs Butcher, having tea in the garden on the oak benches. (*Courtesy of John and Maria Hallam*)

sketches. The original interior photos show much of the studio and bedroom furniture in this simple Arts and Crafts style. Other photos show his use of red brick and a 'preference for sand-faced red bricks instead of the wire-cut and pressed variety'.

Part of the front of St Dunstan's. (*Courtesy of John and Maria Hallam*)

Quennell's 'unfailing dash and gusto' made him a sociable character. It seems 'he danced admirably, attended Bohemian parties given by such members of the artistic avant-garde as … Walter Crane'. It is likely that his and the partners' social circles overlapped, they shared a passion for detail in quality and design.

In 1904 an elegant silver trowel was made to commemorate the laying of the foundation stone of their new home, and after many years elsewhere it has recently returned to grace its original home.

The silver trowel made to mark the building of St Dunstan's, 1904. (*Private Collection*)

A couple of years after designing St Dunstan's, Quennell had a house built for himself in Bickley, incorporating many of the features which had proved so successful at Seymour Place. Like St Dunstan's, 'Four Beeches' incorporated Quennell's characteristic Arts and Crafts features: windows with medallions of stained glass in the mediaeval style, leaded panes and decorative wrought-iron latches and even a large room they too referred to as 'The Studio'. It had folding doors to divide it into two sections as well as the decorative plaster work so popular with Arts and Crafts designers.

The plaster ceiling in Quennell's own studio was embossed with thistles and Tudor roses; St Dunstan's had Tudor roses, R&C initials, a mouse with a long tail, a 1905 date and other decorative squares. These details cannot be discerned in the early photos, and were impossible to make out until the present owner's major restoration. They were painstakingly brought back to their original condition by stripping off many thick layers of old paint.

Details of the plaster ceiling in the studio. Note the R&C initials and the date, 1904. (*Private Collection*)

The panelling and fittings were said to be made by their own craftsmen, and built-in bookcases, window seats, cupboards and shelves can be seen in the photos. Damaged over the years, they too have been restored. Many admiring comments by friends and visitors to their exhibitions are recorded.

A particularly large number of electric light fittings are noticeable in the photographs of the first floor studio, perhaps needed as it was not possible to have windows at the rear, because of the proximity of the adjoining house. Good lighting would have displayed the silver to visitors to best advantage. One of Ramsden's art school awards was for the design of a light fitting and some of those in the studio are very like the one illustrated in *The Artist* in 1902. An obituary in the Sheffield local paper after Ramsden's death in 1939 claimed that Ramsden liked to swing open solid looking panels, with a great flourish, to show beautifully made gold and silver pieces to dramatic effect.

Above: A view of the studio, with the dividing doors open, 1914. (*Courtesy of John and Maria Hallam*)

Left: The entrance to the 'commodious fireplace recess', 1914. (*Courtesy of John and Maria Hallam*)

Their work in a wide range of metals is evident, from light fittings to gates, fire irons, and door and window fittings, all individually designed and crafted by hand. The house still has the superbly wrought iron gates, dated 1904. They were specifically mentioned in the *Sheffield Daily Telegraph*, 'These are entirely hand-forged and welded, and are one of the most notable pieces of modern iron work I have seen'. Originally they had the studio name in wrought iron above them, and the statue above that, as can be seen from the early photo, but they were removed at some time before 1969. It would be wonderful if the name and statue could be found and restored.

The fine hand forged gates at the entrance, 1914.
(*Courtesy of John and Maria Hallam*)

Ramsden's bedroom on the second floor, 1914.
(*Courtesy of John and Maria Hallam*)

Carr's bedroom above the studio, 1914.
(*Courtesy of John and Maria Hallam*)

The work completed, Ramsden and Carr, living and working together, could enjoy the beauty of their home, a wonderful background for displaying their work to potential patrons. The partners shared views on design, and every piece from their workshop carried their joint mark, they always presented a united front to the world. Ghenete Zelleke described their attitude in their early days, viewed by amused contemporaries in 1905:

> Seldom have two artists collaborated so harmoniously as Ramsden and Carr. The pair is inseparable, working together, living together, and always of the same view in all questions of art and life. The effect is almost comical when all questions asked personally of Ramsden or of Carr are answered with 'we'. Ramsden alone or Carr alone has no opinion. 'We' made this or that; this or that artwork in Florence pleases 'us' the most, is always the reply. Then, it happens that either of the inseparable pair has made a tiny physical mistake. Ramsden suffers from nervous blinking of his eyes while Carr reveals his nervousness by stuttering. Certainly 'ego' ['Personalia'] has nothing to do with the art of Ramsden and Carr. [4]

The studio was named St Dunstan's after the patron saint of gold and silversmiths, a popular tenth-century saint who became Archbishop of Canterbury. Creative from boyhood, he is often shown with the hammer and tongs he used in his metalworking. Tradition has it that he used the tongs to tweak the devil's nose. In March 2014 a cast bronze figure of the saint, 37½ inches high made by Ramsden and Carr was sold at auction to an anonymous buyer, it would be good to re-position it in its original place, but in spite of extensive searches its whereabouts remains unknown. It appears to be the figure at the top of the gates which can be seen in the 1914 photograph. An interior photograph within the studio shows a similar statue of the saint. Dunstan seemed particularly important to Carr; on the partnership break up not only did he name his new studio St Dunstan's, but also his country home in Bourne End. His legacy for the building of a Catholic church in that village came with a request for it to be named St Dunstan's, as it is. Ramsden more than once referred disparagingly to another figure of St Dunstan on the staircase of the Goldsmiths Hall which he found particularly objectionable.

St Dunstan's was their home, and a studio only in the sense of a background for displaying their work to customers. Visitors were not encouraged in the Maxwell Road workshop. A recollection in 1984 by Mrs Alison Pierson fifty years later mentioned a small workshop attached to the house, with workmen in leather aprons, but whether this is quite accurate is hard to say.

In the first years Omar and Alwyn, the maid, the cook and the terriers, seem to have lived contentedly there together, working in the Maxwell Road workshop, and building up the business. The commissions kept coming as did favourable reviews. In December 1908 the *Journal of the Royal Society of Arts* reviewed one of Ramsden and Carr's winter exhibitions at St Dunstan's. It wrote admiringly of several rose bowls, jewellery including a gold St George and the Dragon pendant, and a series of Episcopal seals, with one for the new diocese of Polynesia.

> A Gothic mustard pot – one of fourteen executed for the Merchant Taylors Company – is a work that takes rank with the beautiful mediaeval salt-cellars. And mention should also be made of a dignified gold chalice which has been executed for the Brompton Oratory.

The reviewer writes that probably the most interesting feature of the exhibition to many people is:

> The artistic taste and skill which Messrs Ramsden and Carr have brought to bear on the ordinary articles of domestic use. Tea-pots... knives and forks, fire irons, door furniture – for all these they have invented new and charming designs, and their work proves not only that these common-place articles may all be things of beauty, but they may be obtained at a cost little if at all exceeding the prices paid for the ordinary articles which disfigure so many of our houses.

In December 1911 a brief review of 'Arts and Crafts' in the *RSA Journal* mentioned the noteworthy display of metalwork which Ramsden and Carr had shown in their winter exhibition at St Dunstan's. Rather unlike their usual displays it appears there were many smaller pieces as the larger works had been commissioned for the colonies. But the reviewer felt this was interesting as it gave a better opportunity to admire their everyday domestic pieces, toast racks, napkin rings, cutlery and similar. He particularly liked the:

> much more attractive show of jewellery than usual: the small chains were dainty and ingenious in the extreme, and several of the pendants and other more important pieces were really beautiful.

Also in 1911 came one of the many commissions from the Downs Butcher family for a full and expensive canteen of cutlery which the family used and added to over the years. The *Antiques Trade Gazette* said in 2001 that Anne Downs Butcher, later Mrs Omar Ramsden, sold the cutlery, complete with its oak cabinet, after Ramsden's death. An anonymous advertisement in the personal column of *The Times* on 16 December 1943, advertised 'Table silver for sale including fish knives, OMAR RAMSDEN,' perhaps it was Anne's. 'The 336 oz. Service, housed in an oak dwarf cabinet, was sold to Herbert Lingford', formerly Ramsden's accountant, customer and friend. It stayed with the Lingford family (of baking powder fame) for nearly sixty years, until sold for £52,000 by Tennants in Yorkshire in 2001, full sets of Ramsden flatware being quite rare.

Ramsden and Carr's work was mentioned several times in the national press. *The Times* in May 1912 referred to a South African War Memorial being exhibited in the Victoria and Albert Museum. It took the form of a volume containing the names of all those who had fallen. Bound in Nigerian morocco by W. H. Smith and Son, it was enshrined in Capetown Cathedral, behind an 'elaborate metal grille executed by Ramsden and Carr'. They could have had little idea then how many dozens of war memorials they would be making after World War I, which was soon to be upon them.

The Great War would change life for millions, neither Ramsden nor Carr was an exception. In about 1911, the Downs Butcher family came into their lives, soon becoming very much part of the St Dunstan household. It seems probable that they all met and became friendly when Anne Downs Butcher first commissioned work from the firm. The family comprised Charles, his wife Anne, their children Gerald and Joan and the childrens' governess and companion Jeanne Étève. Nearly every post-1912 family photograph shows them all together, Omar, Alwyn, Charles, Anne, Gerald, Joan and Jeanne. There are photographs of them in the garden of St Dunstan's, in Whitstable at their holiday home and on holidays abroad.

The friendship grew but work continued unabated for Omar and Alwyn. In March of 1914, a collection of contemporary British arts and crafts was shown in London, due to be taken to the Louvre in Paris for exhibition. *The Times* reported on:

> the immense strides made in this country during the last fifty years very largely owing to the inspiration and guidance of William Morris and his co-workers. There will be included tapestry, pottery, glass, enamel, jewelry, [sic] gold and silver work, bookbinding, illumination, calligraphy, illustration, furniture, lace and textiles.

Many individual owners lent a wide range of artefacts, including several from Royal collections. It must have been a superb exhibition, the list of exhibitors reads like a *Who's Who* of the Arts and Crafts movement. As well as Morris, his late wife Jane and her sister were represented by embroidery designed by him and worked by them. His daughter May designed and worked pieces of her own. Tapestries designed by Sir Edward Burne-Jones were shown, and work by William de Morgan, Arthur and Georgina Gaskin, James Powell and Sons (now Whitefriars Glass), Walter Crane, Arthur Rackham, Christopher Whall. The listed names are also similar to a membership list of the Art Workers Guild. The recognition of designers and craft workers as artists, including Ramsden and Carr, had really moved forward.

World War I, the Great War, had already begun when Ramsden and Carr produced the leaflet to accompany their November to December Exhibition. It lists and describes a variety of works made before Alwyn left to join the Artist Rifles, including rings, a pendant and bracelet, a motor '*Mascotte*' celebrating speed, the chalice and paten for Whitelands College, a gate of wrought iron and bronze for a 'Kentish seaside churchyard', the '*Lady of Shalott Casket*' and church and city livery company commissions. They also remind readers that they are 'At Home' every Saturday from 3 to 6pm.

SAINT DUNSTAN'S STUDIO,
SEYMOUR PLACE (Fulham Road),
SOUTH KENSINGTON, S.W.

NOV. 26th to DEC. 2nd, 1914 (2 to 6 p.m.)

EXHIBITION

OF HAND-BEATEN SILVER & GOLD WITH ENAMELS
WROUGHT IRON & ARCHITECTURAL FITTINGS

Designed and Executed by

OMAR RAMSDEN & ALWYN CARR.

(*A*) COVERED STANDING SALT in hand-wrought and chiselled silver. Designed and executed for the Worshipful Company of Merchant Taylors by command of C. G. Kekewich, Esq., to commemorate his Mastership of the above Company, 1913-14.
Although based upon a close study of the finest existing examples of historic English silverwork, this Salt is entirely original in design and treatment.

It is 23 ins.-high and weighs 120 ozs. troy. It will be entirely silver fire gilt. The cover is surmounted by a figure of S. John Baptist, the Patron of the Company. In one hand he holds a simple cross light staff and in the other a baptismal shell. The figure stands upon a ball "barry wavy," heraldically symbolic of the waters of salvation.

The knop consists of the clustered Shields of Arms of Kekewich, the City of London, of which Mr. Kekewich is a Lieutenant, the Merchant Taylors Company and the Order of the Hospital of S. John of Jerusalem (of which Order Mr. Kekewich is Knight of Grace).

The base is supported on eight symbolic towers which also carry emblematical figures of the civic virtues, Labour, Justice, Charity, Integrity, Faith, Purity, Hope; and the figure of S. George the Patron of England; the last to mark its having been made in the time of a great War.

(*B*) SET OF JEWELS:—

1. "St. Christopher" Ring in hand-wrought and chiselled gold and platinum.

2. "St. George" Pendant in hand-wrought and chiselled gold and silver.

3. "Tristan and Isolde" Ring in chiselled gold.

4. "Trianon" Ring in hand-wrought and chiselled gold and platinum with emerald and brilliants.

5. Bracelet in hand-wrought platinum and blue moonstones.

Above and pages 98 and 99: The leaflet describing the exhibits in their Christmas exhibition at St Dunstan's, 1914.

C) MOTOR "MASCOTTE." The Conqueror. Figure in bronze and wrought silver symbolizing the conquering of space by speed.

(D) CROZIER. Reproduction of an original staff, part of which was found in an old barn in Kent and presented to His Lordship the Bishop of Rochester, by whose desire it was completed in the 12th century manner from a study of old monastic drawings and existing museum examples.

(E) CANDELABRA in wrought and repoussé silver, with Briar Rose decorations. Part of a large table suite in hand-wrought silver.

(F) ALTAR CROSS AND SIX CANDLESTICKS in hammered and repoussé gun metal and enamel, with crucifix.

(G) MEDAL, in silver parcel gilt, designed and struck to commemorate the memory of Florence Nightingale and to serve as a reward of merit for distinguished nursing services throughout the world.

(H) ALMS DISH in hammered and repoussé bronze and enamel. Designed as a memorial gift to an Irish Church. The centre is decorated with a design of Madonna Lilies taking the general form of a fleur-de-lys and the four panels display various emblematical figures of " Praise to the most High." These panels are connected by a band of Rosemary "for remembrance."

(I) THE "BROUGHAM" LOVING CUP, in hand-wrought and repoussé silver. Designed to commemorate a diamond wedding. The cover is surmounted by the Brougham crest in chiselled silver. The body of the Cup bears the Coat of Arms and an inscription, while the knop has a decoration of diamonds, broom and orange flowers. Underneath the foot is a plate with the names of all the descendants of the recipients.

(J) THE "PULLMAN" ROSE WATER DISH in hand-wrought and repoussé silver. Designed and made for the Worshipful Company of Leathersellers to commemorate the Mastership of Mr. John Pullman 1911-12, and that of his father 1872-3.

(K) SET OF SANCTUARY CANDLESTICKS in cast brass for S. Peter's Church, Lowestoft.

(L) PECTORAL CROSS in wrought repoussé and pierced gold and silver made for His Lordship the Bishop of Hull.

(M) MORSE in wrought silver gilt and precious stones.

(N) LECTERN in cast and hammered brass for a Church in Northern India.

(O) ALTAR CROSS AND PROCESSIONAL CROSS designed and executed for the Church of S. Mary, Alderbury, E.C.

(P) CHALICE AND PATEN. Designed and being made for the Chapel of Whitelands College, Chelsea. It is of wrought silver and enamels with jewels. The stem is decorated with the figures of S. Catherine of Alexandria, S. Cecilia, S. Ursula and S. Martha. An inscription in pierced letters surrounds the foot.

(Q) LOVING CUP AND COVER made for the Worshipful Company of Dyers to commemorate the Mastership of Mr. R. H. Rothwell 1913-4. The body bears the Arms of the Dyers' Company and the lid is surmounted by a swan in allusion to the rights of this Company over the Swans of the River Thames.

(R) ALTAR CROSS, CANDLESTICKS AND VASES for Christ Church, Streatham, in hammered brass and enamel. The centre of the Cross displays the Agnus Dei while the symbols of the Four Evangelists appear as the extremities.

(S) GATE in wrought-iron and hand beaten bronze.

Part of a memorial scheme in a Kentish seaside churchyard.

It is surmounted by a symbolic " tree of life " in forged iron, which springs from a heart shaped panel bearing the monogram " W.G." surrounded with laurel branches.

The higher of the two horizontal bands of beaten bronze is intended to represent "the ever restless sea," while the lower one shows, in symbolic fashion, a submarine cable amid the waves.

(T) CASKET. " The Lady of Shalott."

The enamel panel illustrates Sir Lancelot and his squires riding past the Castle of Shalott on its island in the river. The front displays the City of many towered Camelot. The sides and back contain excerpts from the poem and a suggestion of the river, with its floating autumnal leaves.

(U) CIGARETTE CASKET. " England."

The cover displays in translucent enamel and repoussé and pierced silver some many-towered medieval city where the land and sea meet, the trees and flowers bending for ever under the sweep of the rushing winds.

The sides are decorated with English flowers bound with a ribbon incised with the lines :—

> Buy my English posies !
> Kent and Surrey May—
> Violets of the undercliff
> Wet with Channel spray ;
> Cowslips from a Devon coombe—
> Midland furze afire—
> Buy my English posies
> And I will sell your heart's desire !

(V) CASKET. " Cupid's Fountain " in silver and enamel. " Chant d'amour dans le jardin du Crépuscule," Villa Medici.

(W) ROSE BOWL. "THE ARMADA." (Electrotype reproduction).

This illustrates the running fight up the Channel between the Spaniards and Queen Elizabeth's Fleet.

The Armorial bearings of the following well known commanders are displayed on the English ships :—

Lord Howard of Effingham, Lord High Admiral in the " Arke." Sir Martin Frobisher in the " Triumphe." Sir Francis Drake, Vice Admiral, in the " Revenge." Sir William Winter in the " Vanguard." Sir John Hawkins, Rear Admiral in the " Victory."

The Spanish Fleet is shewn in extended battle array. The " Santa Maria," the " San Phillipe," the " San Fernando " bearing the Royal Arms of Spain and the Arms of the Cities from whence they sailed. The rest of the Spanish Fleet is seen in the diminishing perspective of the half moon shape formation they observed when beating up the Channel. The reverse displays the Royal Arms of Phillip and Elizabeth, surrounded by the orders of the Golden Fleece and the Garter, respectively.

(X) PANEL in translucent enamel " The Annunciation."

(Y) COMMEMORATIVE FAMILY LOVING CUP AND COVER with the Arms of the recipient and his wife.

OMAR RAMSDEN & ALWYN CARR

"AT HOME" in their Studio every Saturday 3 to 6.

This exhibition was to be one of the last before the war. Carr joined the Artists Rifles Regiment in 1914 and Ramsden continued working. The pieces made during the war years of 1914 to 1918 continued to be marked with their joint mark, though Alwyn could have had little to do with their production. Though he was away for much of 1917 a silver book mount still bore their shared mark. *The History of Reynard the Fox* by F. S. Ellis, decorated by Walter Crane, had been published in 1897; it is now part of the Arts and Crafts collection of The Wilson, Cheltenham Art Gallery and Museum.

The Payne family showed a similarly bound book in their *Century of Silver* catalogue of 1989, for the Ashmolean Museum. With it was just part of a personal letter from Ramsden, which Judy Payne had found tucked into the back of a copy of *Reynard the Fox*. He wrote, though it does not say to whom:

> I think you noticed illustrations are by the late Walter Crane who was made Commendatore in Italy and these same illustrations are modelled in hand wrought silver as an outside decoration. Mrs Ramsden bought four copies of *Reynard the Fox* in Bond St years ago. The Ellis edition is now [out] of print. Two copies are now abroad. She has one and this is yours.

Museums Sheffield also has several pieces from this period when Carr was serving in the war.

Whilst Carr was away on active service, Ramsden's relationship with the Downs Butcher family had continued to grow and flourish and by 1916 the family was living at St Dunstan's. Omar had not been called up, he was forty-one when war broke out; he was either over the age for conscription when it was introduced in 1916 or not physically fit, we don't know. But certainly, by 1916, the whole family had moved in permanently, exactly why remains a mystery, but presumably they were all happy with the arrangement, though their home in Cottesmore Gardens was less than a mile away. When Gerald went to Harrow in 1916, records show his address as St Dunstan's.

Since their lives became so integrated with Ramsden's, and he and Anne eventually married, the Downs Butcher family story is of some interest. Charles Downs Butcher was born in 1867 in Whitstable, a fishing town on the north Kent coast, still famous for its oysters. His sister's grandson David has related stories about the family; their ancestors on both sides had been mariners, oystermen and hovellers in Whitstable for several generations. Amongst other marine work, hovellers salvaged goods from shipwrecks. The family story tells that Charles's maternal grandfather Joshua Downs was one of the few who really struck lucky, this is confirmed by his rapidly improving social position. He became one of the richest men in Whitstable when he and a partner found a hoard of sovereigns in a wrecked ship. Joshua invested his new wealth wisely, buying shares in several boats, properties in Whitstable, and becoming solidly middle class. Of his three daughters, Hannah Downs married Robert Butcher, from another local family of mariners who also had shares in boats, the usual way for them to be owned.

Robert's father had gone to sea as a boy in 1830 and worked his way up to the position of Captain, acquiring his Master's Certificate, or 'ticket'. Robert too was very drawn to the sea and would spend as much time as he could with boats and gazing out to sea from the shore. But by the time he was married to Hannah Downs and had a couple of children, she wanted more security than a mariner's life allowed, having no wish to join the long list of Whitstable widows. The families on both sides had lost boats at sea, sometimes with the loss of all the crew.[5] It seems that Hannah's now wealthy father set up his son-in-law Robert in one of his properties, an ironmonger's shop in Oxford Street, next to the East Kent Hotel, which is still there. Robert became an unwilling shopkeeper rather than a mariner.

Hannah and Robert had six children, three boys and three girls, of whom Charles was the second. All the children were given their mother's surname of Downs as a middle name, Charles was the only one to attach it to his surname. The Downs family was now well established and known in the town. Joshua was firmly Wesleyan, holding official positions within the chapel in addition to his several properties and his boats.

Frustratingly, family photographs of the generation of Charles' parents are unnamed, but everyone is beautifully turned out and appears prosperous. His father retired to West Cliff, and there are photos of all the family in the back garden.

Charles was known as Billy in the family circle, which would have made him Billy Butcher as a child, much less dignified a name than Charles Downs Butcher. He was to create a business and become a wealthy man, doubtless with his ambitious wife Anne spurring him on. His working life started modestly in London, in 1891 he was a drapery assistant, living with dozens of other single employees at 19/20 New Bond Street, apparently accommodation for staff who worked in a large department store. Then as now Bond Street was a fashionable and expensive shopping area. Just a little further up the road at 10/20 Vere Street Anne's younger sister Jessie was living in a similar situation as one of dozens of young unmarried dressmakers, milliners and drapers' apprentices and assistants, male and female, part of Marshall and Snelgrove in Oxford Street. Possibly that was how Charles and Anne met, they married in 1893 in St George's, Hanover Square. It was eleven years before their son Gerald was born in 1903, followed in 1907 by a daughter, Joan.

Charles's career flourished, by 1901 he had moved up from drapery assistant to drapery buyer and was living in a handsome late Victorian terrace in Putney with a domestic servant. By 1903 when his son was born Charles had made the major move into self-employment, and proceeded to build up a very successful cloth manufacturing business. In a family legal document of 1906 Charles is of 'The Cottage, Horsmonden, Kent, Gentleman.' A family photo shows him and young Gerald standing at the door of the pretty cottage near Tunbridge Wells which seems to have been an early country retreat.

Annie Emily's family also came from Kent. Called Dolly by her family, she soon dropped that and later changed 'Annie' to 'Anne'. Born at 66 Broad Street, Northgate, Canterbury in 1871, she was the daughter of Charles James Berriff, a coach trimmer like her brother, grandfather and great grandfather of Marylebone. Her father had moved from London to Kent, married a local girl and they had seven children; Annie had five brothers and Jessie, a younger sister. She always told her own children that she was descended from silk weavers in Bruges, and a drawing of a house in Bruges was kept on the wall to suggest this. The house in Canterbury where she was born is a great deal more modest, being a very small terraced house.

In fact, her Grandmother Berriff and two Berriff aunts were employed as coach lining makers in York Mews in Marylebone, which appears to be the closest connection with silk. There is no evidence of any earlier history in Bruges, but her grandchildren say that Anne liked to embellish the story of her family background. As far back as 1790 her paternal ancestors were coach trimmers in Marylebone, her great grandfather having moved there from Leicestershire, so no suggestion of interesting foreign ancestry. Her maternal grandfather had been a thatcher in Kent.

By 1911 Charles, Anne and the children had moved upmarket again from Putney to Kensington. On the census night they had left eight-year-old Gerald there in the charge of his nurse and the cook while Charles, Anne and Joan visited his parents in Whitstable. At that time he was a manufacturer of dressing gowns, and family members recall talk of his fabric business in the City near Bow Bells (St Mary le Bow).

As noted already, the first traceable commissions which the Downs Butchers gave to Ramsden and Carr were about 1911, a napkin ring for Joan, aged five, and the large canteen of cutlery already described. By now Annie always called herself Anne, though she signed official documents in her baptismal name of Annie Emily. A handsome bracelet was made for her with her name on it, and a ram's head at one end, but the present owner was told that Anne did not like it much as she thought it too ornate.

Anne's bracelet, decorated with a ram's head, by Ramsden (and Carr?) which she
did not much care for. (*Private collection*)

The discovery of early photographs, in an album marked 1914, was
exciting, giving a wonderful view not previously known of the original
interior and garden of the house and its occupants. They confirm the
family intimacy of Ramsden, Carr and the Downs Butchers before World
War I. The album must have belonged to Carr and is probably the one
mentioned in a letter from Alwyn's nephew to the late Paul Hallam.
They show a comfortable looking group of family, friends and dogs,
and Alwyn in his Artists Rifles uniform. Having volunteered for the
war in 1914 he was away much of the time, presumably there was now
room for Charles, Anne, Gerald, Joan and Jeanne. The arrangement
must have suited everyone except Alwyn. The Downs Butchers were
still comfortably off then, commissioning expensive silverware
and jewellery. Around that period, Charles acquired Graystones, a
handsome holiday house in Whitstable, and one of the first telephone
numbers in the town, *Whitstable 87.*[6] The road, Borstall Hill, is now
completely built up, but at the time it was just a country lane within
walking distance of his parents. I managed to identify the house with the
invaluable input of local people, yet another instance of the help I have
been given to solve the many small mysteries of the search. Margaret
Lewis traced the Downs Butchers to Borstall Hill from the 1923 Blue
Book or local directory held in the Beaney Library, Canterbury. Mike
Butcher, a distant cousin of Charles who had found the early phone
number, photographed the house. He found that the old barn in
the background of the early photos was still just about standing, and
managed to take a photo of it just before it was demolished in 2016.

The Downs Butcher family in the rear garden of Graystones, with Carr and Ramsden, pre-1919. (*Courtesy of Simon Gilmore*)

The extended Downs Butcher family, plus Carr, Ramsden and frequently Jeanne Étève, often spent time there, enjoying the sea air and visiting Charles's family. They could have travelled quite easily from London, either by train or driven by the chauffeur which they now appear to have acquired. The photo taken in the back garden of Graystones, against the old barn, confirms their visits, they had brought in a professional photographer to record themselves as a group. The four family members can be seen with Omar and Alwyn. Gerald looks about fifteen and Joan about eleven, which would date the photo to near the end of the war.

By now, Alwyn was becoming unhappy with the domestic arrangements. It was at this time that the rift between the partners, which ended in their parting, was developing. Ramsden appears in all of the photographs to be completely relaxed, smiling, (always smoking) and at the centre of the Downs Butcher family, whereas Alwyn appears much less comfortable.

He must have stayed at St Dunstan's when home on leave, an early photo shows him in uniform in the garden. But he was evidently unhappy with this domestic arrangement and in the end the decision was made that he should move out and the partnership be dissolved. He had known Ramsden closely for twenty-five years, studying and travelling with him and sharing accommodation and business. The decision to part was presumably mutual, but must have affected his life in a major way, much more so than Ramsden's. The photos show Omar fully enjoying his adoptive family life, the children called him 'Uncle Chirpy' as he talked a lot and was very animated in the family circle. Joan always said that, unlike her own mother, he was unfailingly kind to her, and photographs always show them looking completely comfortable together. This view of him, both from family reminiscences and the photographs is quite different from the accounts of him in the workshop, which came from Leslie Durbin, where he was considered a stern disciplinarian, talking only of work and keeping his family life private. There is little doubt that Alwyn resented the changes and had been happier with the pre-war household of just himself and Omar. Anne was by most accounts a domineering woman and Alwyn may have felt excluded or diminished. There is a sense that he just went along with the wishes of the more assertive members of the group. In December 1918 Ramsden entered his own separate mark in the London Assay Office; he had already marked a silver chalice and paten of 1918 with it. The momentous decision had been made to end the partnership of twenty years.

With Carr's departure from the business and from St Dunstan's, life continued and so did the exhibitions. *The Times* of 3 December 1921, still carried an advertisement in the Art Exhibitions section, for a four-day viewing of Ramsden's work 'hand- wrought in Gold and Silver, from 3 to 6pm only.' Sometimes Ramsden sent personal invitations to friends or potential customers.

Charles, Joan and Omar to the rear, Alwyn, Jeanne and Gerald at the front, *c*1916.
(*Courtesy of Simon Gilmore*)

In the chauffeur driven car, Joan, Omar and Charles, undated.
(*Courtesy of Simon Gilmore*)

A family photo, Jeanne, Joan, Omar and Charles, undated.
(*Courtesy of Simon Gilmore*)

Omar and Gerald, undated.
(*Courtesy of Simon Gilmore*)

A winter holiday abroad in the 1920s, Joan, Omar and Gerald, undated.
(*Courtesy of Simon Gilmore*)

Omar and Joan, about 1920. (*Courtesy of Simon Gilmore*)

As late as 1929, there was enthusiastic praise for the studio: The Sheffield newspapers continued to write about Omar's activities from time to time. Under the heading, 'ONE OF "SWEET NELL'S" MULBERRY TREES' was an article by a journalist who had obviously visited St Dunstan's:

> Mr Omar Ramsden … lives in one of the most delightful houses in London. It stands in a little side-street off Fulham Road, S.W., on a site which was once Nell Gwynne's mulberry garden. Part of that garden still remains, and in it still flourishes one of 'Sweet Nell's trees.
>
> Commodious Fireplace Recess: The house is full of old oak-panelling. Its biggest room is Mr Ramsden's studio, but not his workshop. Its walls are entirely covered with oak and its lofty ceiling also.
>
> In a deep recess in which about a dozen people can sit in perfect comfort there is a remarkably fine fireplace which has been built up with odd pieces of old stone and wood panelling 'picked up' by Mr Ramsden during his wanderings on the Continent.
>
> Several large glass cases in the studio are filled with lovely examples of Mr Ramsden's art – goblets, chalices, plates, candlesticks, cups, and other objects wrought in silver and gold.
>
> Door with a 'Peep-hole': The main door of the studio-house is approached by way of a wide loggia with a red-tiled floor. The house itself might be that of a monastery. It is of stout oak and is fitted with a little sliding panel as a 'peep-hole'.

During the years after Ramsden's death, St Dunstan's suffered many depredations. At some time the large studio was divided into two, and a minstrels' gallery added to the dividing wall. Later, in 1963, songwriter Lionel Bart, then at the height of his success, bought the house and submitted plans for extensive alterations, decorating it in an eccentric personal style and installing a bar, cinema and sauna. He referred to the house as 'The Fun Palace', using it as a base for entertaining his show-biz guests, said to have included The Beatles, the Rolling Stones, Terence Stamp, Noel Coward and others. The 1966 World Cup winning team held their post-match party there. Bart himself said, 'Because I was such a peasant I had some of the very heavy Pre-Raphaelite stained glass windows taken out to let in more light. I gave them to a bricklayer'. Noel Coward described the property as 'not so much a house, more of an amusement arcade'. About 1970 Bart sold the house, he was declared bankrupt in 1973.[7]

From 2009 to 2011 the house was totally restored by its new owner in a major undertaking, in which quality and longevity were made priorities. Arts and Crafts features were carefully brought back to as near the original as is compatible with modern living and comfort, a considerable achievement, especially as the early photographs were unknown at the time. Handmade solid oak panelling was restored, fireplaces rebuilt, and the decorative plaster ceiling completely refurbished. The stained glass roundels in the windows were taken apart, the lead calms replaced, and the whole set with hand-blown glass. The oak window frames were remade and hand-wrought iron fittings added. Though Ramsden and Carr might have been horrified at the condition of St Dunstan's in the 1970s, they would have been impressed by its restoration in the twenty-first century.

1 London County Council Planning Application 902:1904, Kensington and Chelsea Archives.

2 *Sheffield Daily Telegraph*, 5 December 1903.

3 *The Marble Foot*, Autobiography by Peter Quennell, Collins, 1976

4 *British Art: Recent Acquisitions and Discoveries at the Art Institute. Omar Ramsden and Alwyn Carr: An Arts and Crafts Collaboration*. Vol.18, no.2, Ghenete Zelleke, Curator of European Decorative Arts, The Art Institute of Chicago. 1992 pp167–180. Copy PHA

5 Letter 24 May 1979 from Wallace Harvey to David Barton, unpublished.

6 1919 and 1920 Phone Directory, Whitstable, Kent. www.oystertown.net

7 111A *Seymour Walk*, Kathryn Sylvano, privately published for CC Construction Ltd, 2009

CHAPTER 6

Captain Carr's Life, During and After the War

Many people initially greeted Britain's decision to join the war in Europe on 4 August 1914 with great enthusiasm. Men were encouraged to join the army through newspaper articles, posters, songs and speeches, they responded in their thousands, keen to do their duty. It was widely felt that a militaristic Germany was oppressing the small country of Belgium, and that the British would put her in her place, defending principles of justice and fair play. Lord Kitchener's request for 100,000 volunteers was oversubscribed; within eighteen months he had two million. Later, as the number of casualties mounted the eagerness diminished and conscription had to be introduced in 1916.

Alwyn must have been one of those convinced of the worthiness of the cause. Although he was forty-two, he volunteered in October 1914 as a private in the Territorial Force, the 28th London (Artists' Rifles), generally known as The Artists' Rifles. A territorial force was not officially required to serve overseas, only in home territory, replacing men from the regular army who were sent abroad. Carr's personal qualities must have been evident and he was soon promoted to Corporal.

In October 1914 the first of the three Artists Rifles Battalions was mobilised as the 1/28th County of London Battalion and became one of the first territorial regiments to serve abroad as a fighting unit voluntarily. The regular army of the British Expeditionary Force had just endured:

... colossal losses in the 7th Division ... we had suffered fearful casualties, and the proportion of losses in officers was higher than in any other rank...I was suffering almost agony, to know where I could get officer reinforcements. You all know how any fighting force must...deteriorate badly, unless this supply of officers is kept up properly and regularly.[1]

Commander in Chief of the British Expeditionary Force, Field Marshal Sir John French visited the Artists Rifles and asked the Commanding Officer to select fifty of his men to be commissioned immediately to partly replace the losses. So after extremely brief training the 'first fifty' of the Artists, as they became known, were made up to 2nd Lieutenants (the most junior officers) and went straight into action leading regular army soldiers.

Their competence and courage were greatly appreciated by the Commander. The scheme was found so successful that the role of the First Battalion evolved into that of an Officer Training Corps, both in France and England, and they were soon turning out one hundred officers per month. Once officers were trained and commissioned they were sent to other Regiments and Corps throughout the army, which is how Alwyn arrived in the Royal Army Service Corps, where by April 1915 he was made a Second Lieutenant, then Lieutenant. On 5 June 1917 he was Gazetted Captain, but the next year was shot, and invalided out on 15 July 1918, though keeping the honorary rank of Captain. His promotions are recorded in the Roll of Honour.

Of the 15,022 Artists who served during World War I, Alwyn Carr was one of 10,256 who were 'Gazetted to Commissions.' The 1922 *Artists Rifles, Regimental Roll of Honour and War Record*, 1914 to 1919, recently reprinted, provides a complete list of all officers and other ranks in the regiment, and all the commissions and honours they received. 2,003 were killed in action or died, 3,250 were wounded or gassed, 532 were recorded missing and 286 became prisoners of war.

It has proved impossible to find more details of Alwyn's war experiences, although his years in the military obviously meant a great deal to him and his wartime experiences must have affected him profoundly; he referred to himself as Captain Carr for the rest

The Artist Rifles Roll of Honour, 1919. (*Front cover of facsimile book*)

of his life. At the beginning of the Regimental Roll of Honour is a photograph of the memorial to all the Artists who lost their lives. One of Alwyn's first post-war commissions was for the central bronze panel of this memorial at the Regimental Headquarters in Duke's Road. It is no longer there, the building is now the centre for the Contemporary Dance Trust. Where is the memorial panel now?

Central panel of the Artist Rifles war memorial panel, designed by Carr, 1919.
(*From a copy of a facsimile book*)

In 1921 Captain Carr was again commissioned to create a decorative silver casket to contain the Regimental Roll of Honour presented to Colonel H. A. R. May on his retirement. May had formerly commanded the regiment and continued his association with it. After his death, his widow presented the silver casket and Roll to the Artist Rifles Association, with whom it remains.

The casket designed and made by Carr, 1921.
(*By courtesy of the Artists Rifles Association*)

The regiment had been formed in 1860 as part of a Volunteer Rifle Corps in response to a fear of French invasion under Emperor Napoleon III. First known as the *38th Middlesex (Artists) Volunteer Corps.*, by 1889 they had permanent headquarters at 17 Duke's Road, Euston, where their name, by then the *20th Middlesex (Artists) Rifle Volunteers* can still be seen with their emblem in terracotta tiles above the doorway.

The earliest members were mostly painters and sculptors; Sir Frederic Leighton RA was a founding member and one of its first Commanders, he remained an Honorary Colonel and the Artists provided a Guard at his funeral. The élite membership reads like a list of Pre-Raphaelite painters, including John Everett Millais, Dante Gabriel Rossetti, Edward Burne-Jones, William Morris, W. Holman Hunt, Val Cameron Prinsep, Ford Madox Brown, Luke Fildes, poet Algernon Swinburne and sculptor Sir Hamo Thornycroft; even the great John Ruskin was an honorary member.

Members had to buy their own kit, the uniform costing £3 8s 4d.

Entrance cost half a guinea and the annual subscription was one guinea. Drills were taken seriously and held eight times monthly, in the rather decorative pale grey uniform they had selected for themselves. Leighton's uniform is displayed in the Leighton Museum. The physical requirement does not sound very onerous; men had to be at least 5 ft. 3 in. with a chest measurement of 32 in. minimum.

The present Artists Rifles Association has a fascinating collection of memorabilia, unfortunately without a home at present, some of which was exhibited in Hampshire in 2014, to commemorate the outbreak of World War I. It includes a drawing by Theodore Blake Wirgman of the unit relaxing on the grass in Wimbledon after a days' skirmish in 1880. This may be the drawing that Thornycroft displayed in the hall of his own house, 2 Melbury Road, which gave rise to a writer from *The Strand Magazine* to note, 'he [Thornycroft] and Sir Frederic had the biggest heads in the corps, and there was always a great difficulty in getting the regulation helmets to fit'. The National Portrait Gallery has a preparatory pen and ink sketch of Thornycroft for the group drawing.

The regiment's emblem, shows Minerva and Mars and their motto 'Cum Marte Minerva', suggesting the desirability of an alliance between war and wisdom. The ribald verse that follows is said to have been popular with members: 'Mars he was the God of War, he didn't stop at trifles. Minerva was a b.... whore and hence the Artists Rifles'.

In the early days the group seems to have enjoyed particularly lively and sociable meetings, which culminated in their founding the Arts Club in 1863, to separate social from military life, it is still active today. Captain Carr followed in the footsteps of the earliest members in several ways. As a student in Sheffield his work had been judged by some of them in national competitions. He joined the regiment they had formed, and after the partnership with Ramsden had broken up he moved into Sir Hamo Thornycroft's former studio at 2 Melbury Road, an exclusive area renowned for its successful artist residents.[2] In 1935 he was invited to membership of the exclusive Arts Club they had established. Many were, or had been, members of the Art Workers Guild, as Carr was.

Although early membership was made up of painters, poets, engravers, musicians, actors and sculptors, later The Artists Rifles included professional men. In 1893 less than five percent were artists, though they have always kept the traditional name. Membership comprised roughly twelve percent architects, twelve percent lawyers, ten percent doctors and six percent civil engineers. The level of education was much higher than average, most men came from public schools or universities. The apostrophe in their name was dropped in 1937 as it was so often misused.[3]

Although often creative and artistic, there was no suggestion that the men of the Artists Rifles were in any way effete as soldiers. They received a particularly high number of honours and other awards for gallantry, often gained after moving on from the Artists to other regiments. The public school ethos encouraged courageous and brave leadership though it brought about a much higher than average casualty rate amongst young officers in World War I.

Over The Top, a painting by John Nash (see page 120) now in the Imperial War Museum, shows men of the 1st Battalion Artists' Rifles in 1917 moving from their trench near Cambrai directly into the machine gun fire which killed sixty-eight of the eighty men within a few minutes. Nash was one of the twelve survivors. Rifles men contemporary with Alwyn Carr included Nash's brother Paul, also an official war artist, Alfred Leete who created the image of Lord Kitchener which evolved into 'Your Country Needs You', and poets Wilfred Owen and Edward Thomas, both killed in action.

By the time Alwyn was invalided out of the army in 1918, he had served for four years and risen to the honorary rank of Captain. His brother records that he was ill for several months but when recovered he attempted to 'throw himself again into the collaborative work of the old partnership, with which, in spite of his military duties in France he had endeavoured to keep in touch…' By the time he returned, the

'Over the Top' by John Nash, depicting the Artists Rifles going 'over the top' on December 30, 1917. (*Imperial War Museum*)

Downs Butcher family had been living there for several years and this was not at all to Alwyn's liking. One imagines that he was resentful, seeing them as intruders.

Although it must have been a major step for Alwyn to leave his home of fifteen years, it appears that in the end it was the best course of action for him. It seems likely that he came into his own more easily once he was away from that grouping and out of the shadow of the extrovert Ramsden. Before long he developed a deep friendship with Arthur Henry Hughes and in time they moved in together, living discreetly and amicably together until Alwyn's death in 1940.

His brother Arthur Carr wrote of Alwyn that 'according to his own estimate he found this the period of his richest and fullest production'. Unfortunately, there is no full record of his work after the partnership.

But by the time he wrote his will twenty years later it was obvious that whatever feelings of bitterness he had formerly held towards Omar, they were by then all forgotten and forgiven.

It took until the spring of 1919 for the partnership to be formally dissolved; Ramsden had already marked a few pieces with his individual mark by 1918. Alwyn moved just a mile away to 2a Melbury Rd., Holland Park, into Sir Hamo Thornycroft's former studio, which he maintained for the rest of his life.

St Dunstan's Studio, 2a Melbury Rd., Alwyn's home and studio from 1919 to the end of his life, formerly belonging to the Thornycroft family, 2016. (*Author's photo*)

Several of the original artist occupants still lived in the road; Marcus Stone RA at number 8, Sir Luke Fildes RA at Woodlands, number 11, and the Holman Hunt family at number 18. The area around Melbury Road and Holland Park Road had been established as a prestigious artists' neighbourhood in the latter 1800s. Many early Artists Rifles men had had houses built near to Sir Frederic Leighton's, now the Leighton House Museum, where his ceremonial sword and other items from his early command of the Rifles are displayed.

Like other artist homes and studios nearby, the Leighton House windows faced north; being extremely large they provided good light and enabled huge canvases to be moved in and out. A separate entrance was made for models to come and go, Leighton considered it unseemly for them to use the main entrance. Next door lived Pre-Raphaelite painter Val Cameron Prinsep RA. His studio similarly took up much of the first floor and had two very large north facing windows, though he did not feel the need for a separate staircase for models. Much of his early life had been spent at Little Holland House across the rear of his new garden, a gathering place for an intellectual and creative élite. His aunts included art photographer Julia Margaret Cameron and Marie, grandmother of Virginia Woolf and Vanessa Bell; friends and visitors included the famous Alfred, Lord Tennyson and Charles Dickens. When this large house was demolished, a studio/house for popular painter G. F. Watts RA was built on part of the site. At the age of forty-seven Watts married actress Ellen Terry, aged sixteen, although she did not remain part of the Melbury Road set for long, leaving him after less than a year of marriage.[4]

Other wealthy Victorian artists had houses and studios in the area designed for them by renowned architects; Marcus Stone's was designed by R. Norman Shaw; several of those who formed the Art Workers Guild had been trained in his offices. Stone was another friend of Dickens, illustrator of *Little Dorrit* and *Our Mutual Friend*. Shaw designed another house for Luke Fildes, illustrator of Edwin Drood. Such was the fame of Fildes that King Edward VII decided to visit to sit for his portrait and greatly admired the house. Latterly it became home to the late Michael Winner, then to singer Robbie Williams. Next door is the unusual Tower House, designed by architect William Burges for himself, now owned by Jimmy Page, guitarist of Led Zeppelin.

Other previous owners included poet John Betjeman and actor Richard Harris. William Holman Hunt wrote his memoirs in number 18 in 1903, looking down towards the Leighton House gardens. So now, as then, the area is home to the rich and famous and Alwyn would have been very appreciative of the cultural connections. The roads were wide and tree lined, adjoining Holland Park, and the detached houses were handsome with large gardens. When Alwyn moved into Melbury Road, it was to a highly regarded neighbourhood, which was no doubt a salve to his pride. His next door neighbours in 1923 were still Sir Hamo and Lady Thornycroft, who had had a pair of large adjoining houses, 2 and 4, built across the garden from their friend Leighton's house; this incorporated several studios for artistic family members, including the large studio at the side which became Alwyn's home. He named it St Dunstan's, like the studio he had just left in Seymour Place. The Thornycrofts let the house adjoining Alwyn's to a Mr and Mrs Russell Barrington, 'who felt this was indeed a delightful opportunity of entering the highest precincts of art under the most helpful auspices', such was the reputation of the neighbourhood. Let us hope that Captain Carr felt the same way. He certainly felt a connection with his neighbour at number 2, bequeathing his 'statuette of Siegfried' to her in his will.

Hamo Thornycroft, RA was well known for statues of such public figures as Oliver Cromwell, situated outside the Houses of Parliament, and Alfred the Great at Winchester; his smaller works still grace private drawing rooms. His sister Teresa was the mother of Siegfried Sassoon. Though Alwyn was of the generation following these artists one imagines he was happy to inherit the prestige and cultural heritage of the area. It was considered quite good enough for Queen Mary to visit him there in the 1920s. Today, many of the original artists' houses bear English Heritage Blue Plaques and a walk around the area next to the

Leighton House museum shows several of them, with their huge studio windows.

The Electoral Register of 1923 shows Alwyn living alone at 2a Melbury Road, aged fifty-five.[5] But by this time he was friendly with Arthur Henry Hughes. By 1925, they were intimate companions and lived together here and in Berkshire. Alwyn must have recovered from the war and from the distressing break with Ramsden and he began to work productively on his own account. While Ramsden was happily enjoying family life with the Downs Butchers, Alwyn too created a contented domestic life of his own with Hughes.

Much of the information about Alwyn's partner Arthur Hughes has come from his brother's great grandson, Tom Hughes. Alwyn, or Captain Carr, as he was always referred to in the Hughes family, was on very friendly terms with family members.

Arthur had been born in the High Street in Rowde, Wiltshire in 1890, fourth of the six children of the local blacksmith James Hughes and his wife Mary Ann. An article, possibly from *The Wiltshire Gazette and Herald* (found in Paul Hallam's archive) on Arthur's death in 1970 gave some details of his life, not mentioning, of course, his homosexual relationships:

> A former apprentice with the *Wiltshire Gazette* at Devizes, who became a partner in a firm of printers in London, died on Saturday … with his three brothers he was a member of Rowde Church Choir and became an apprentice compositor in Devizes on leaving school. He then became a journeyman – compositor in Marlborough before going to London. Mr Hughes was a writer of short stories and poems as well as a watercolour painter … he was the last survivor of the Hughes family. Two of his brothers were killed in action in the 1914-18 war, and a third died in 1945 from wounds received during the war, in which he was taken prisoner.

Arthur was the only brother who did not fight in World War I; he was thought to have a heart defect, though in fact he lived to the age of eighty while all his brothers died young. He worked for the Royal

Printers, Eyre and Spottiswood, who, amongst other things, printed sporting magazines. The family believes that this is where he met Alwyn Carr, eighteen years older, who contributed articles on shooting. Alwyn attended the wedding of Arthur's brother Leonard with him; in 1925 a daughter Betty was born. Alwyn made a christening cup for her, beautifully engraved with flowers and her name, which she kept for about eighty years. Betty told me the story of the day her mother went to Captain Carr's studio to help him prepare for a visit from Queen Mary. She helped lay out the velvet on which to display his silver to best advantage. Alwyn is remembered as enjoying the companionship of the Hughes family, much more so than that of the Downs Butchers, where he seems to have been overshadowed.

Until recently Arthur's cigarette case, with his initials engraved on the front, remained in the Hughes family. It has the joint Ramsden and Carr mark, the Birmingham assay mark and a 1902 date. As far as is known, Alwyn and Arthur did not know each other then; the most likely explanation suggested for this early date is that on the dissolution of the partnership in 1919 the existing stock was divided between the partners and Carr took some of the cases which had much earlier been bought from Birmingham for later personal engraving. The cigarette case was recently sold at auction to a collector from a family who were early customers of Ramsden.

Arthur Hughes cigarette case with the Ramsden and Carr mark, probably 1902. (*Private collection*)

It took me quite some time, and a lot of help, to unravel the details of Alwyn's life in the country after 1919, and his death and burial there. Unlike Omar, he showed no apparent interest in publicising his work and activities. After the partnership breakup Omar's name came up several dozen times in *The Times* in connection with his work, whereas Alwyn's name was mentioned only once. This was in April 1939, only a year before his death, and was not related to his work, but as Captain Alwyn Carr he was on the published list of Box and Stall subscribers for the season at the Royal Opera House in Covent Garden. The majority listed were titled people including an Earl, Lords and Ladies, Viscounts, Barons and Countesses. He obviously liked to sit amongst the aristocracy when he went to the opera.

His will, made when he was sixty-six in 1938, was the most helpful document I came across in bringing an understanding of his life, family and friendships. It covers nearly twelve pages, including a three-page codicil added five days before he died in 1940. In it he gave his own address as Melbury Road and his companion Arthur's as Watersmeet in Theale near Reading.

Perhaps this is discretion to avoid mentioning their living together. But Betty Hughes remembers Captain Carr and her Uncle Arthur sharing a country home at Watersmeet before they moved to Bourne End in about 1934. The Hughes family has a photograph of Arthur in the garden there against a background of sweet peas, and another of

Left: Hughes family photo of Arthur in the Watersmeet garden and Alwyn and Arthur on the river, with another of the terriers. (*Courtesy of the Hughes family*)

them both, with a small dog, boating on a river (though this is undated).

When I managed to find Watersmeet, it turned out to be a lovely house in a delightful rural situation which is virtually an island, where the River Kennet meets the Kennet and Avon Canal.

Watersmeet, Theale, near Reading, 2015. (*Author's photo*)

A few years later Alwyn bought a large plot of land for a house on the Abbotsbrook estate in Bourne End, Buckinghamshire, closer to London and near the Thames. Abbotsbrook itself is a distinctive forty-five acre planned estate mainly built in the Arts and Crafts style between 1898 and 1907, on the site of a mediaeval nunnery. A most attractive conservation area now, it was laid out around streams, green verges, hedges and trees, each house being individually designed. As a private gated estate, with houses on spacious plots, there are very few cars to be seen on its roads even now, adding to the peaceful rural feel.[6]

Carr had this third St Dunstan's built about thirty years after the original houses, so is not in the same Arts and Crafts style. Its name was

Carr's country home, which he named St Dunstan's, now renamed, 2015.
(*Author's photo*)

changed when the last of the Carr family left and there seemed no way
of knowing which of the dozens of houses it was today. Walking around
the estate looking for clues, local people were very helpful, the trail
went from Andy, the postman, who suggested that Colin and Susan
Cleugh knew a lot about the history of the estate and might know, so
he directed me to their home. They kindly invited me in, disturbing
their breakfast, and searched their papers, but as their knowledge
was primarily about their own house, they were unable to help. They
suggested that Ken Townsend, local historian, might be more likely
to know, so I crossed Bourne End to find him, disturbing him at his
gardening. He too searched his own notes in vain for a reference to
St Dunstan's, he advised me to ask Jan Parkinson of the Abbotsbrook
Residents Association. She helpfully sent an enquiry around the
members until, at last, someone knew which house had originally
been named St Dunstan's, and what it was called now. Success! After

contacting the owners they were happy to show me the house and garden. About half of the plot, where Alwyn's tennis court had been, had been sold off, but a large plot remained. The late Betty Hughes owned a watercolour painted by her uncle Arthur Hughes of a small bridge over the stream immediately opposite the front garden. The view of the bridge is virtually the same today.

Watercolour by Arthur Hughes, showing the view from the front of their house, much the same today, *c*1930s. (*Courtesy of the Hughes family*)

Resident David Baldwin searched through old papers and in the 1907 Schedule of Plots, he found that the double site which Alwyn had bought was Lot 33, plots 73 and 74. On the 1925 plan the plots were still vacant. David's further searches in the Trustees Minutes Book for 11 November 1934 show the beginnings of Alwyn's house: 'Plans have been passed for the erection of a new house by Mr Richards on land purchased from Captain Barclay'. The next year, 1935, 17 November, the minutes read: 'The new house, St Dunstan's, owned by Captain Carr, was assessed at £700, due, 21/–'. [7]

It was now possible to picture Alwyn and Arthur, living companionably here and in London. Alwyn continued to work actively on his own account, though it is much more difficult to find examples of his post-war work than Omar's. As already noted, he carried out several commissions for the Artists Rifles soon after the war. *Who's Who* 1936 lists some of his work over the years, adding that he designed and executed many memorials to commemorate the thousands lost in World War I. The Imperial War Museum is collecting data on as many of these memorials as possible, including the names of the designers and makers. Several works by Ramsden are listed, but no memorials by Carr are identified. Details of their ordering and making would only be found now by searching individual parish or diocesan records for the years following 1918.

Who's Who recorded that he had designed and made the East and West gates within an architectural scheme for Wellington College in Berkshire. It mentions too his work for several public bodies, including the Thomas Gray Memorial Shield for Navigation, awarded by the RSA. He created memorial cups for Admiral Tufnell and Henry Leaf, and silver vases for Winchester College Chapel. In 1919 he was asked to make a memorial cup for Sir John Furley, who had played a major role in founding the St John's Ambulance Association in 1877, and had early involvement in the Red Cross. Furley was knighted for his:

... life-long humanitarian involvement in military medical matters and designed a stretcher [the Furley stretcher] and the wheeled version known as the 'Ashford Litter' after his birthplace in Kent.

In 1916 he was presented with another Ramsden and Carr bowl by his old friend W. J. Fieldhouse to commemorate his eightieth birthday.

1920 brought Alwyn a commission from physicians at St Bartholomew's Hospital for a silver vase and cover, which they wished to present to Sir Archibald Garrod on his leaving the hospital for another position.

Who's Who also noted his 1924 commission for six candlesticks and an altar cross for the Lower Chapel of Eton College. The cross was a gift from Arthur C. Benson, and the candlesticks were presented by Lady Powell in 1925 in memory of her brother, C. F. Wood. He had been a pupil at Eton but drowned in an accident in 1869 during the summer holidays. The set is still in regular use. Much of Alwyn's work at this time seem to have been for churches and hospitals. No doubt his wartime experiences had affected an already sensitive man, and he would have had a particularly sympathetic approach to memorial commissions.

Candlesticks and an altar cross for Eton College, 1925. (*Reproduced by permission of the Provost and Fellows of Eton College*)

The information comes from the 1990 exhibition catalogue of the commemorative display of silver, 550 years after the founding of the college:

> According to the notice in *The Eton College Chronicle* (25 June 1925) 'The cross and candlesticks have been most skilfully adapted from a carefully chosen pattern by Captain Alwyn Carr: and Mr W. W. Watts contributed his great knowledge in the selections of model and material and supervised the details of all the work.[8]

William Walter Watts had served for many years as the Keeper of the Department of Metalwork at the Victoria & Albert Museum. The present Keeper, Eric Turner, described the influence on the candlesticks of fifteenth and sixteenth century North Italian prototypes, and the cross as having 'stylistic affinities with a series of late 14th and 15th century North Italian processional crosses in the V&A'. He considered that 'it demonstrates that Carr was thoroughly accomplished in absorbing and interpreting traditional subjects'. His versatility enabled him to make innovative designs as well, an example being the modern silver vase for Winchester College which he showed in the *Exhibition of Modern Silverwork* at Goldsmith's Hall in July, 1938. The vase was designed by Professor RMY Gleadowe, which would have ensured its being 'a design of pre-eminent modernity'.[9]

In 1930 a fine pair of gates designed and executed by Carr was formally opened by His Royal Highness Prince Henry, Duke of Gloucester, at the Royal National Orthopaedic Hospital in what was then Edgware, now Stanmore. The photograph shows details of the gates, with the angel heads blowing trumpets at the top. In 1929 an anonymous donor had offered £1,000 for the provision of gates at the entrance to the hospital, and Carr was commissioned. The opening ceremony took place on Buttercup Day, September 1930. The wording on the gates is from the sixth verse of *The Divine Image*, part of William Blake's *Songs of Innocence*: 'Where Mercy, Love and Pity Dwell There God Is Dwelling Too'. Carr seemed to have a gift for choosing beautiful and apt wording, like this quotation for the hospital and the one for his own gravestone.[10]

Opening ceremony of the gates of the Royal National Orthopaedic Hospital, by the Duke of Gloucester, 1930. (*Courtesy of Derek Sayer, Historian, Royal National Orthopaedic Hospital*)

In 1935 Alwyn was invited, as Captain A. C. E. Carr, to membership of The Arts Club, having been proposed and seconded by existing members, confirming that he continued to enjoy appreciation and respect fifteen years after his break from Ramsden. It was a private gentlemens' club formed as mentioned by members of the Artists' Rifles, where men from the worlds of art, literature and science could meet socially. Early members had included many Royal Academy painters including Lord Frederic Leighton and Sir Hamo Thornycroft whom we have already encountered in the Holland Road/Melbury Road group. John Tenniel, illustrator of *Alice in Wonderland* and influential *Punch* cartoonist was a member; the elegant club rooms would sometimes appear as backgrounds to *Punch* cartoons. From the earlier literary world had come Charles Dickens, Anthony Trollope and Rudyard Kipling. Foreigners were occasionally allowed, usually as temporary members, they included Mark Twain, Monet, Rodin, and Degas.

G. F. Rogers wrote a history of The Arts Club in 1920, describing the luxurious premises and listing the Holland Road artists and the Art Workers Guild members. Walter Crane's name appears with a short reflection on him. He:

> was distinguished in many branches of Art ... he was perhaps best known for the interiors of buildings ... An ardent and convinced Socialist he was somewhat combative and eager to promulgate his own views.[11]

The club kept their first premises for thirty years, until moving to 40 Dover Street, Mayfair in 1896. They managed to survive the problems of two World Wars, even the horror of the replacement of male waiters by women, who 'set a somewhat exaggerated value on their services.' Today, members still gather in Dover Street, attracting such famous names as Grayson Perry, Ronnie Wood, Gwyneth Paltrow, Beyoncé and Jay Z.

Throughout the later 1920s and 30s, Carr maintained an affectionate relationship with staff and students at Whitelands College, now part of the University of Roehampton. His friendship with them became evident when I looked more closely at the clause in his 1938 will, wherein he left them £100 for their May Queen Cross and Chain Memorial Fund. When I visited the university I was shown lots of relevant material in their abundant Whitelands archive.

When it opened as a teacher training college in 1841, Whitelands was the first institution in England to offer higher education to women. It was situated on the King's Road, Chelsea, just a short distance from St Dunstan's. The obituary published in the College Annual on his death in 1940 described Carr's long connection.[12]

The idea for instituting an annual May Queen festival had evolved from the friendship between John Ruskin and College Principal John Faunthorpe; the Whitelands Archive has the correspondence between the two about the form the event should take. The Queen was to be chosen annually by her fellow students, as 'the lovablest and the likeablest' girl'. (Ruskin's words.) Ruskin took a great personal interest in the college, using his friendship with William Morris and several of the Pre-Raphaelite Brotherhood to enlist their help in beautifying the ugly college chapel. This resulted in a wonderful set of windows designed by Edward Burne-Jones, a magnificent reredos and other decoration by Morris. The windows can be seen today, reset in the present university building. Ruskin was very generous in donating copies of his own and others' books, and pictures and gifts to the college, in order to add to the beauty of the young women's' surroundings. These were to encourage and develop their aesthetic appreciation and to bring them to an understanding of his views on the nature of beauty and its relation to the spiritual. Following her election the May Queen would hand out copies of his books to her attendants, his writings were popular so the books were prized.

After the first few years each May Queen had a dress specially made for her to wear on the day; the college archive includes a fascinating collection of dresses from the first one in 1881 to the present; a selection of these are regularly on display. Former May Queens are invited back to each yearly festival, and their dress is kept for them, they were designed to allow for later expansion! In some more recent years, a May King has been chosen.[13]

The May Queen also received a handmade cross and chain to keep as a memorial, this is where Alwyn Carr was involved. As it is customary for these to be returned to the college on a Queen's demise, the college now has a good collection of them.

The first two crosses, for 1881 and 1882 were designed by Arthur Severn, husband of Ruskin's cousin. Burne-Jones was asked to design the 1883 cross, but apparently Ruskin did not care for it as the May Queen's botanist father criticised it for inaccuracy. The design returned

Photographs of former May Queens and their attendants, wearing their crosses and chains, 1921. (*By kind permission of the Whitelands College Archives, University of Roehampton*)

to Severn until Ruskin's death in 1900. Canon Rawnsley then took over responsibility for the crosses until his own death in 1916, having them made by the Keswick School of Industrial Art, well known for their Arts and Crafts work. Mary Birch, a student then Governess at the college, took great interest in the ceremony and at her death in 1916 left a fund for future crosses and chains. This is the fund to which Alwyn Carr bequeathed £100.

It seems probable that Carr and Ramsden's first connection with the college came in 1914 when they were commissioned to make a chalice to commemorate the life of Kate Stanley, Head Governess for many years. The College Annual of 1915 describes and illustrates it:[14] Like every other piece from their partnership years, the Stanley Memorial Chalice has the joint 'R&C' mark, making it impossible to know which of the two was responsible for the design. But as it was Alwyn who maintained the relationship with the college it seems quite likely to have been him.

15

The Stanley Memorial Chalice.

(THE ARTISTS' DESCRIPTION).

THIS magnificent and massive Chalice and Paten which is presented to the College Chapel as a memorial to Miss Stanley, has been designed and executed by Omar Ramsden and Alwyn Carr, in hand-wrought, chiselled and repoussé silver parcel gilt. It is of very large size, being 13 ins. high, and weighs 93·30 ozs. troy. The bowl, which is plain, fits into a calix of vine leaves, stems and fruit designed, as indeed the whole work is, in the spirit of English Gothic art, but with distinct modern feeling and detail.

Intertwined in the vine is a ribbon or label with the Latin inscription :—*Calicem Salutaris accipiam et nomen Domini invocabo.* Underneath this calix is a large fiery carbuncle (presented by Mrs. Faunthorpe) set in gold and protected by the upward growing stems of vine from which the calix springs. The knop is formed of a band of pierced vermeil thorn work over translucent enamel, and interspaced with carbuncles.

This knop is supported by a cluster of four canopied niches, forming the stem of the Chalice. In these niches are four figures of saints, modelled in the round and highly chased and chiselled. First is placed the name-saint of her to whose memory the Chalice is dedicated ; S. Catherine of Alexandria, Patroness of Education and Colleges. She is crowned to show her royal birth and holds the palm of martyrdom and the Holy Book.

S. Martha, Patroness of Housewives, is shown holding the pot of Holy Water and the Asperge with which she conquered the Tarasque or Dragon, which is seen lying at her feet, the symbolism of which needs no explanation. A bunch of house hold keys hangs from her waist.

S. Cecilia, Patroness of Music, bears in one hand the palm of martyrdom, and in the other a symbolic Organ.

Finally, our own Patron Saint, to whom our Chapel is dedicated. S. Ursula, Patroness of Women, devoted to the education of their own sex, is crowned and has an ample mantle with which she enfolds three young girls. As a king's daughter she is richly apparelled and holds two arrows, the instruments of her martyrdom in one hand.

The base is very spreading in character, is formed of six concave sides, and bears in letters in high but delicate relief the following inscription :—

Dedicated to the Glory of God in memory of Catherine (Kate) Stanley, Head Governess of Whitelands College, 1876-1902. At Rest, May 31st. 1913.

FROM THE ARTIST'S DESIGN.

Drawing and description of 'The Great Chalice', c1913. (*By kind permission of the Whitelands College Archives, University of Roehampton*)

'The Great Chalice'. (*By kind permission of the Whitelands College Archives, University of Roehampton*)

The 1992 Ruskin Lecture states that it was Ramsden who made the first few crosses, possibly until the partnership dissolved in 1919. He was later replaced by Carr, whose designs continued until 'fairly recent times'.[15] [written 1992]

He was so excited by Ruskin's tradition that he designed little presents for the May Queens from himself and entertained them to tea in his workshop when he presented his small gift. One such was a wonderful St Christopher medallion which he gave to Queen Kathleen in 1936.

On the reverse of the medallion Carr has engraved, 'Whosoever looketh upon the image of Saint Christopher shall not faint nor fail on that day'.

Carr left instructions for the design and making of future crosses and chains. Leslie Durbin made the 1951 cross, though it seems possible that Carr's designs were used right up to 1985 when Andrew Lammas took over.

In January 1967 letters between Shirley Bury, Keeper of Metalwork at the Victoria & Albert Museum, and Miss Ker, the College Librarian, indicate that Miss Ker had asked for help in identifying the makers of 'the great chalice' from their mark. Mrs Bury supplied details of Ramsden and Carr, and a few remarks about them. This particularly beautiful example of the work of the partnership was still of interest to the museum curator and to those responsible for its care in the 1960s, illustrating that good design has an enduring beauty.

1 *Artists Rifles Regimental Roll of Honour and War Record, 1914–1919* Preface, Earl French, pxi, Howlett and Sons, London 1922, Third Edition. Facsimile: The Naval and Military Press, (undated)

2 *The Holland Park Circle*, p180, Caroline Dakers, Yale University Press, 1999,

3 www.artistsriflesassociation.org/regiment-artists-rifles.htm

4 British History Online, *The Holland Estate: since 1874*, pp126–150, Survey of London: Vol.37, Northern Kensington. Originally published by London County Council, 1973.

5 Electoral Roll, 1920, 1921, 1923 Kensington Directories

6 www.abbotsbrookconservationarea character survey

7 Abbotsbrook Trustees Minutes, November 1934 and 1935

8 Exhibition catalogue, 550th Anniversary of the founding of Eton College, Sotheby's, 1990, p29. Eton College Archives.

9 *Masterpieces by Omar Ramsden from the Campbell Collection*, Catalogue by Lynne Springer Roberts, Introduction by Eric Turner, pp16–17, David A. Hanks & Associates, Inc., New York, 1992.

10 Derek Sayer, Historian, Royal National Orthopaedic Hospital, Stanmore.

11 *The Arts Club and its Members*, GAF Rogers, Truslove and Hanson, London, 1920 Facsimile, p12.

12 *Sisterhood of Queen Ellen*, obituary of Captain Carr and reply from his brother to letter of condolence, 1940 Whitelands Archive, University of Roehampton.

13 RBKC *libraries blog* (Royal Borough of Kensington and Chelsea), *The May Queens of Whitelands College*, Dave Walker, Local Studies Librarian.

14 1915 *Whitelands College Annual*, drawing and description of cup. Whitelands Archive.

15 *Ruskin Lecture 1992, 'Be Like Daisies'*, Malcolm Cole, Brentham Press for the Guild of St George. Whitelands Archive.

CHAPTER 7
Ramsden's Life After the War

Once Alwyn had moved out of St Dunstan's in 1918, Omar and the Downs Butchers' family lived there in a comfortable familial relationship. Omar was continually busy with his work, lectures and articles, arranging exhibitions and discussing commissions with clients. Anne is thought to have been a good organiser, helping both her husband Charles and Omar with their business arrangements. Gerald went from Harrow to University College, Oxford and Charles ran his successful textile business. As well as holidays abroad, they would all visit Graystones, the Downs Butchers home in Whitstable.

In the immediate post-war years, both Ramsden and Carr were commissioned to create dozens of memorials to the thousands who had been killed or wounded. One of the earliest, in 1915, was an unusual Royal Artillery Regiment Commemorative photograph frame, following the death of a young soldier, Norman Donaldson, at Neuve Chapelle, an early British offensive which brought heavy casualties.

Memorials took a variety of other forms. In 1918 three members of the Carpenters Company in Throgmorton Avenue in the City of London presented something rather unusual to their Company, a silver rosewater dish. Ramsden described it in one of his talks ten years later:

> That is a memorial tablet. It has taken the form of a rose water dish. It is a memorial to three young men killed in the war, subscribed by their fathers, who, I think very rightly, thought it would be nicer to have something cheerful to remember them by rather than a plaque on a church wall.

The dish is inscribed as being made '…that there may be brotherly remembrance of their sons…' It was presented at a Court on 4 February 1919. Almost immediately Ramsden was allowed to borrow the dish for an exhibition at the Royal Academy. One of the bereaved fathers, the current Master, David Wintringham Stable, presented another cup and cover to the Company, on January 12, 1926, 'as a memento of his year in office'.[1] Two more pieces were commissioned from Ramsden in 1933, to commemorate the 600 years of their '*Boke of Ordinances*' of 1333; these were a Master's Badge of white gold and precious stones and a silver rosewater dish for the '*Master, Wardens and Commonalty of the Mystery of Freemen of the Carpentry of the City of London.*'

On St George's Day, 23 April 1919, one of the earliest public memorials was unveiled in the church of St George the Martyr in Canterbury. The solid bronze tablet was in memory of the officers and men of the Dover Patrol Flotilla who had lost their lives in the naval action at Zeebrugge in 1918. It is on a background of oak taken from one of the flotilla. In the town of Dover a memorial service continued to be held annually on 23 April for many years.[2]

In 1920 Omar was commissioned by the Consulting Surgeons of the British Army to make a silver gilt mace for presentation to the American College of Surgeons, 'In memory of mutual work and good fellowship during the Great War'.[3] The model for the mace was a mortar dug up from a trench in Salonika.

A more conventional memorial to fallen soldiers from the London Hop Exchange was unveiled in 1922 by Brigadier General Wigan, who had been involved in the hop trade. *The Times* published a photograph of the unveiling ceremony at the exchange in Southwark Street on 22 January. The wall plaque by Ramsden lists the names of the dead, and can be seen on the wall of what is now the Slug and Lettuce pub, at 32 Borough High Street.

Just over the road from the memorial is an attractive building with terracotta decoration in the Arts and Crafts style showing idealised hop pickers. It belonged to *W. H. and H. Le May, Hop Factors*; one of their sons is listed with the dead. This area of Southwark was a major centre for dealing in the hops needed for the brewing process. Being on the south-east side of the city there was good access to the hop fields of

Kent. It is well known that hundreds of East Enders, men, women and children, decamped there annually to bring in the harvest.

Sandwich in Kent has a fine memorial from 1922 outside St Peter's Church, showing St George on horseback killing a dragon, a frequent theme with Ramsden in sizes from this one to cigarette cases. The plaque is mounted on a brick screen and is a bronze relief, 100 mm deep. Side plaques list the names of the eighty-seven men from the town who died.

War Memorial outside St Peter's, Sandwich, naming the eighty-seven men from the town who died. 2016. (*Victoria Hendrick photographers*)

The parishioners of St Luke's Church in South Park, Reigate, Surrey, commemorated their war dead with a complete chapel within the church. The Imperial War Museum is currently looking for information in order to compile a listing of all war memorials in the country; who designed and made them and whose responsibility it is to maintain them. The south wall of St Luke's is listed as having a memorial rather unusual for Ramsden, a silversmith and art metal worker, in that it is simply constructed in oak and painted with the names of the nineteen dead, on a blue background. There is no silver or other metalwork on the plague. Frustratingly, the Imperial War Museum information does not explain how Ramsden's involvement came about.

Memorials were still being made six years after the war. In 1924 barristers from Lincoln's Inn commissioned a bowl to be set on their table.[4] It bears this inscription: 'To commemorate the barristers who dined at this table and gave their lives in the War, A.D. 1914–19'. It is set on a plinth made of wood from the HMS *Monarch*: It has been ordered and ordained that whenever the bowl is placed here, two seats on each side of the table, representing one mess, shall always be left unoccupied'. The tradition continues today.

Domestic life was ordered and stable and photos show Omar to be a close member of the family unit. Another valued member of the household (and, like Omar, not a blood-relative of the Downs Butchers) was Jeanne Clemence Victorine Étève, governess and companion to Joan. Always called Tante Jeanne in the family, she was responsible for the childrens' faultless French. Included in many of the family outings and photographs, she was remembered by her charges and their own children with warmth and affection. Anne Downs Butcher, later Ramsden, greatly favoured her son Gerald over her daughter and Jeanne gave Joan the maternal affection she lacked. Jeanne was careful not to voice any criticism of Anne as a mother, but seemed to understand Joan's need, and they remained close friends for years. Joan's older children remember Tante Jeanne very fondly, relating how she never forgot their birthdays even when she went back to live i

France. She returned to England from time to time specially to visit them, taking them to Harrods for ice cream and treats.

In addition to her role in the family, Jeanne was a skilled enameller; his workbooks show that she undertook work for Omar in the early 1920s, once the children had less need of her. Alwyn had carried out some enamelling in early partnership days though his skill was limited, and since his departure in 1919 there would be a need for an enameller in the workshop. Several fine pieces have been attributed to Jeanne, including in 1921 the *Four Seasons or Mother Earth Casket*. Her payment is shown in a sheet of paper inserted into the workbook, 344 hours at 1/1d per hour, making £18 12s 8d altogether. This is one of the few occasions when Ramsden recorded the time he spent himself on the design. For comparison, while Jeanne was paid 1/1d hourly, Ulyett, the manager, was paid 2/6d per hour for the drawing, and Martin was paid 2/– per hour for the chasing. Ramsden calculated his own contribution at 'say' just over £2 in total, for the design and supervision. He wrote a note at the bottom of the page to the effect that, although the casket could reasonably be sold at 40 guineas, it was well worth 100 guineas. He was right to think that it was a highly desirable piece; it continues to be highly valued today. It appears to have been made for stock, there is no mention of its being commissioned.

In the same year a Jewel Casket, Order 782, is attributed to Jeanne. There is no record in the workbook to confirm this; if it was loose like the one above it seems quite likely that it got mislaid. Similarities of style between all three mentioned here are so marked that it is widely accepted that they are by the same hand. The silver has a 1921 date mark, and the casket, with a lock and lined with velvet, was a present for ᴏuisa Poulton from her husband George, a shoe manufacturer from ᵗhamptonshire.

next year, 1922, Jeanne carried out the enamel work on a ᵘnted plaque on a chain, described as the '*Large Stella Maris* ᵉ workbook records that she spent one week on a spoiled ᵘd it took about three weeks to carry out the complex design. Again, Ramsden recorded his own time spent with Ulyett in the drawings.[5] The name in the presentation case suggests it was sold through Asprey, goldsmiths and jewellers to Queen Mary.

Stella Maris Enamel, enamel work by Jeanne, 1922.
(*The Wood Hall Collection, image courtesy of Hancocks*)

Jeanne was highly skilled, whether she had that ability before she came into the household is not known, and why she stopped enamelling remains a mystery. Joan, her charge, was fifteen by 1922, so was less in need of a constant companion. Jeanne was a witness to Omar and Anne's marriage in 1927, so obviously was in London then. It has been speculated that as she had spoiled one attempt Ramsden did not want her to do more work, but that seems very unlikely, since the second attempt was so successful. She is thought to have carried out secretarial duties at home for Ramsden for a time, and the photographs and stories show that she was very much part of the family. Ramsden had provided very generously for her and Joan in his will, in the event that Anne died before him. She returned to France in due course, but a search for her name in France in the capacity of enamel worker has been fruitless. Later in the 1920s and 1930s Omar used the services of Henri W. de Koningh for enamel work. De Koningh designed and made jewellery in London on his own account but also carried out fine enamelling for other silversmiths.

In 1920, Charles took Gerald abroad, travelling First Class on the P&O Line from Gibraltar. He was now a Company Director and business was obviously doing well. One wonders whether he had benefited financially from supplying cloth for war purposes. He continued to commission more expensive items from Ramsden, possibly at Anne's behest, including a silver cup in 1922 and a gold and diamond pendant for Anne the next year. In 1924 Gerald celebrated his twenty-first birthday and Ramsden's order book shows that a cigarette case and a ring were made for him.

Around this time two undated orders appear to show that the Downs Butchers were creating a grandiose family history for themselves. They commissioned a fire screen with the Berriff and Downs Butcher arms; Ramsden would have had to be very inventive to create these for families who had originally been hovellers, an ironmonger, coach trimmers and a thatcher. In 1924 a silver teapot, sugar bowl and milk jug and in 1925 two gilt frames were ordered, so Charles' business still flourished at this stage. One of his grandsons now owns a bookcase ornamented with the letters CDB, with rather a nautical look, reflecting Charles ancestors and the family's maritime history.

As the numbers of war memorials gradually decreased more secular commissions came Ramsden's way. He was consistently busy, undertaking work for livery companies, churches, cathedrals as well as making domestic pieces. He was a member of various groups including the Goldsmiths' Company, the Royal Society of Arts, the Art Workers Guild and others, producing lectures and articles for these and other bodies. His work was exhibited widely, in Leeds, Liverpool and Birmingham, as well as at the Royal Academy and other galleries in London and North America, and it was reviewed regularly in the art press. In 1921 he became a member of the Royal Miniaturist Society, whose exhibitions included crafts as well as paintings. The largest size allowed for a work was 8 inches (20 cm) in height; so several of Omar's smallest works qualified for display. According to their 1921 catalogue, for example, his exhibits that year included four 'Saints' spoons, a claret jug, silver goblets, jewelled rings and a cigarette case. He was invited to join the Royal Miniaturist Society Council where he stayed until at least 1936, often exhibiting his work.

In 1925 his exhibits there included the *Girdle of the Pilgrim's Way*, thought to be the one his wife later wore; and a cigarette box with the long name of *'Cigarette Casket, Sir Walter Raleigh's Ship bringing home*

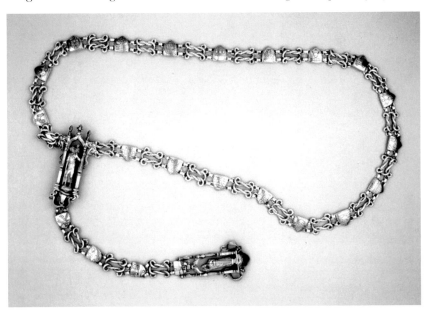

Girdle of The Pilgrim's Way, depicting St Christopher carrying the Christ Child, and the shields of the towns along the way. Often worn by Anne Ramsden, about 1924. (*British Museum Images*)

the First Load of Tobacco, Arms of Queen Elizabeth and Sir Walter Raleigh on the Sail'. In 1930 he showed the copper model for the famous *'Jewel and Collar of the Honourable Company of Master Mariners, as worn by HRH The Prince of Wales, The First Master, 1929,'* which brought his invitation to visit the Prince at St James' Palace. Unfortunately bombing during World War II destroyed the Royal Miniaturist Society office and their records, what remains of their catalogues are held in the Arts Library of the Victoria & Albert Museum.

In 1925 Omar was commissioned to make the first of several items for the Parish Church in Whitstable, the town of Charles' birth, where they now enjoyed their seaside retreat.[6] In 1937 Omar was called in again to complete a major re-ordering of the east end of the church, by designing communion rails, a reredos, cross and candlesticks.[7] He was brought in after a previous scheme had been thrown out 'after years of negotiation with the Faculty Board'. The work can be seen by arrangement in situ today.

Ramsden exhibited in the Liverpool Autumn Exhibitions right through the 1920s and 1930s.[8] The catalogues make interesting reading, showing the wide range of goods displayed, and their current prices in guineas. One year his works included another silver and enamel casket priced at £22 10s. This may be the one bought for the Cranbrook Academy of Arts in Michigan

Wrought silver and Whitefriars glass scent bottle, undated. (*Private collection*)

and taken to the USA. A *'Scent Bottle in Wrought Silver and Whitefriars Glass Rose and Lily Design'* was priced at ten guineas.

The next year's show included his *'Old King Cole'* Sweetmeat Box, in hand beaten silver, jewelled with chalcedony, costing seventeen guineas. The catalogues held by the Walker Gallery indicate that not all the pieces he showed were for sale. Most works were priced, but he was known to borrow back larger more interesting pieces he had already sold, to make a more dramatic display at selling exhibitions. For example, the *Hanworth Cup*, or *Cumberbatch Trophy* presented by the writer's Great Aunt Alice Cumberbatch as an aviation trophy was exhibited in Liverpool in 1934, as was the nef, *The Good Ship St Andrew*, of 1928. Many of the smaller pieces displayed in Liverpool were for domestic use, such as jugs, bowls and vases, though he included a Processional Cross in 1926, priced at one hundred guineas. Cigarette boxes were decorative as well as useful, and Sir Walter Raleigh, with his association with tobacco, was a popular motif. 1923 showed a less expensive variation, the *'Sir Walter Raleigh Ship'* at ten guineas. Ramsden might change the name of a work for a different market. He continued to exhibit in Liverpool until his death.

In 1922 Ramsden produced *The Dream Ship*, a very impressive work of extraordinary detail.[9] The sails are beautifully enamelled, and painted with Neptune, indigenous North Americans, African tribesmen, Inuit and a Viking. The ship was commissioned for Mr and Mrs Henry Ford by Sydney Houghton, thought to have been an interior decorator in Manchester Square. He prepared a leather album of photographs of the hull and sails which suggest he was the designer. If this was the case he and Ramsden must surely have discussed the feasibility of making up such a design from a silver craftsman's point of view. Ramsden's Special Order Workbook (Order 890) show that a loss of £31 1s 6d was made on the ship; it appears that the price he had quoted did not cover the extra work which Houghton added later, presumably Ramsden felt unable to charge for it. The ship was sold from Mrs Henry Ford's estate in 1951 for $625. The identity of the enameller has never been completely established; although this was certainly the period when Jeanne Étève was carrying out enamelling for Ramsden the techniques used are quite different from those on the caskets known to be her work.

The Dream Ship, 1922. (*Courtesy of Ralph Holt*)

The next year another superb ship or 'nef' was made.[10] In May 1923 *The Times* reported in detail the gift of the major work now known as *'The Sir Percy Cox nef'*, presented to him and Lady Cox on his retirement. The work made by *'Omar Ramsden of Kensington'* was commissioned by the British Chamber of Commerce in Baghdad, Basra and Mohommerah. Sir Percy Cox had served for years in the military then the government in the Middle East, particularly in Mesopotamia (now Iraq). The area was crucially important to British interests as a source of oil, particularly for their navy, and Sir Percy played a central role in enabling successful British commerce there. The impressive retirement gift was commensurate with the work he had carried out for years in protecting British political and commercial interests. He had major responsibility for drawing up the boundaries of the new Iraq and instituting Feisal as an acceptable king to the many conflicting parties in 1921. The British remained there by agreement as advisers and colleagues. In his speech at the farewell banquet Sir Percy said that 'the new Iraq government was a child and they were bound for a time to look after its interests even more than their own'.

Appropriately, the nef was a merchant ship, with full rigging and sails, and according to *The Times* it was in the form of a replica of *The Ship of Good Fortune*, though it is not clear what ship this is. Ramsden's workbook shows careful costing in code for the ship, which amounted to £210 14s 0d, since the first had caused such a loss to the business. His workbook entry is a good source of general information once decoded. It shows which craftsmen worked on which parts of the complex piece, including Ulyett, Coles, Massey, Martin and Best, for how many hours, and the hourly rate of pay for each man, according to his skill. It records that the oak base was made by Rogers and Co., who normally carried out all the work in wood which Ramsden needed. The total weight of silver used was 184 troy ounces (nearly 6000 grams) and it took a surprisingly short time to make; no doubt it was easier to make the second having so recently made the first. It was ordered on 13 December 1922 and finished on 27 February 1923, a matter of just eight weeks.

On 19 January 1923, a selection of work from the Royal Academy's Winter Exhibition was illustrated in *The Times*. In addition to Ramsden's chalice and paten the whole page is of interest in evoking a sense of the time. It shows two very fashionable gowns in the style Ramsden's customers might have worn, and a betrothal photograph of the Duke and Duchess of York, later to become King George VI and Queen Elizabeth. They were presented with a claret jug the following April by the 'the artist in metalwork, Mr Omar Ramsden' as a wedding gift from the Royal Academy whose members had selected the gift 'as a work of modern craftsmanship'.

One of his most important Royal commissions came in 1926, when Ramsden was selected, after a great deal of discussion, to design and make a large silver gilt alms dish. About eighteen inches in diameter, it was planned as a gift from King George V to the new Cathedral of St John the Divine in New York. The Public Record Office in Kew holds fifty-six detailed pages of correspondence concerning the dish in Foreign Office files of 1926 and 1927. They show the numerous discussions over what form the gift should take, whether it was to be a present from the Government or the king, whether the money allowed by the Treasury for the bowl (at first £50) was enough. In the end Ramsden suggested that £75 ought to be allowed for a work of sufficient quality, and this was granted. The means of selecting the right artist/craftsman had been another matter of concern. It was decided that the Director of the Victoria & Albert Museum should be involved; he recommended seeking the advice of the British Institute of Industrial Art. Its chairman, Sir H. Llewellyn Smith approached Omar for a design, and reported back 'that he was a first-rate artist and interested in the proposed work'. The much admired 1926 Ascot Cup was cited as an example of his skill.

The King duly approved the chosen design and the dish was made. Before the alms bowl was sent to the USA Ramsden was able to display it in his usual Christmas Exhibition at St Dunstan's. One of the few surviving letters in his own handwriting accompanied an invitation to Mr and Mrs G. K. Menzies to visit the exhibition, and mentions that he would particularly like to show them the 'important work on view which I have just done for the King'.

ST. DUNSTAN'S,
SEYMOUR PLACE (FULHAM ROAD),
SOUTH KENSINGTON,
LONDON, S.W. 10.

Station :
SOUTH KENSINGTON.

Telephone :
KENSINGTON 6629.

PLEASE QUOTE
No. .... November 17th 1926

Dear Menzies,

It seems absurd to think you have not been to see me all these years and at the risk of seeming a bit "pushing" I enclose a Card for my next "Show". Needless to say, I shall be very pleased to see you and your wife if you care to come.

I shall have some important work on view which I have just done for the King and which I should like you to see.

I also enclose a booklet on "mags" of which I have been guilty and which I trust you will do me the pleasure of reading at your convenience.

Yours sincerely

Omar Ramsden

S. DUNSTANS. SEYMOUR PLACE, S.W. 10
The entrance to Seymour Place is in Fulham Rd near the Boltons

G. K. Menzies Esqre
+ friends

OMAR RAMSDEN requests the pleasure of your company to view an Exhibition of his Works on Thursday Nov. 25th, Friday Nov. 26th Saturday Nov. 27th Sunday Nov. 28th 1926 The Exhibition will be open from 3 to 6 p.m

An invitation to Mr and Mrs G. K. Menzies, asking them to visit his exhibition, 1926. (*Private collection*)

Ramsden holding the silver alms dish made for George V to present to the Cathedral of St John the Divine, New York.

It was sent in the Ambassadorial bag to New York in early January 1927 and arrangements made for its presentation by the British Ambassador on the King's behalf. His Majesty expressed a personal wish that no publicity material or exhibition would appear before the presentation as this would 'detract from the originality and to some extent the dignity of the gift.' The ceremony took place on Sunday, 13 February 1927 and was widely reported in the *New York Times* and other newspapers throughout the United States. The cathedral archives hold extensive material relating to the occasion, covering the guests, the celebrants, the description of the bowl, the speeches made and the thanks conveyed to His Majesty. *The Times* in London also wrote a full descriptive article in February, illustrated with a photograph of Ramsden in St Dunstan's studio, holding the bowl. His clients, including Mr and Mrs Menzies, who would have seen the bowl at the Christmas selling exhibition, were rather privileged to see it before it was taken to New York, given the King's express wishes about publicity. Perhaps the edict about keeping the work on a low profile had not reached Omar, as it seems unlikely that he would have gone against the wishes of his distinguished patron. The Christmas exhibition was, after all, a semi-private affair.

The story goes that there was controversy over whether it was appropriate for the King to commission so expensive a bowl in 1926, when Britain was suffering economic depression, high unemployment and the General Strike. During the Strike, which lasted nine days from 4 May to 13 May, the Foreign Office wrote on 12 May that the King would consider the submitted designs after 'the present emergency'. In the end King George was said to be very pleased with the dish when Ramsden was personally invited to take it to the palace. The story also says that Ramsden was quite a favourite of both Queen Mary and King George, and produced several works for the Royal family.

But on a personal front, in the next year, 1927, life changed radically for the family group. After many years of financial success for Charles, his manufacturing business collapsed and went into receivership. It may have been the result of the national economic depression of the later 1920s, but no doubt the anxiety caused contributed to his ill health. On 25 July, Charles died in a nursing home, he was only sixty. He and his family had lived with Omar at St Dunstan's for over ten years.

He died from heart disease and endocarditis in Peckham House Nursing Home in Camberwell. I wondered why he had been there, so far from home, on the other side of London. Looking into it, I found that Peckham House had been founded as a 'Lunatic Asylum' in the nineteenth century, London Metropolitan Archives believe it remained an asylum until it closed in the 1950s, taking paying patients as well as paupers. No records from the asylum survive, so it is not possible to say whether or not Charles was suffering a mental breakdown of some kind, perhaps consequent on his business collapse. The Grant of Probate to his wife Anne showed that his financial worth was 'nil'.

Only three weeks after Charles' death his widow and Omar had the first Banns of Marriage read in the Anglican St Augustine's Church, Kensington. On 3 September, less than six weeks after the death, Omar and Anne were married.[11]

By any standards, this was very soon after Charles death and has inevitably caused speculation. Anne was officially penniless after enjoying years of a comfortable lifestyle with Charles; marriage to Omar would have brought her financial security. On Omar's part, it made official the family life which he always enjoyed, and it would have seemed more conventionally respectable to be married since they now lived as single people in the same house. It would seem to be an arrangement which suited them both admirably, rather than a love affair. Anne's granddaughter says they were always the greatest of friends though the marriage was never consummated; Anne 'hated that sort of thing'. There was no evidence that he was homosexual, even though he had been a close friend and business partner for over twenty years with Carr, who developed a life-long relationship with another man after the business partnership with Ramsden had ended. At the time of their marriage, Omar was fifty-four and Anne was fifty-six, although she gave her age as fifty on the marriage certificate. Their witnesses included Anne's son Gerald, Jeanne Étève and Newman, who carried out secretarial and other work for Ramsden; they can be seen in the background of the wedding photo.

Marriage of Omar Ramsden and Anne Downs Butcher, 3 September 1927.
(*Courtesy of Anne Wells, Anne Ramsden's granddaughter*)

Joan was devastated by her father's death as they had always been close. She was in France, aged twenty, when his death occurred but Anne refused to allow her daughter to return home for the funeral, insisting she stay abroad. Possibly she did not want to hear any objections to her imminent re-marriage. If Charles had indeed died in a state of mental distress, perhaps Anne wanted to keep it from Joan.

Omar and Anne enjoyed a happy marriage, travelling extensively together: to Sweden the year after they married, to Scotland in 1932, to Berlin, Ravello and Rome in 1933, to Athens, Istanbul, Damascus, Syria, Israel and Norway in 1934, and to Austria and Germany in 1935. Omar cited foreign travel and the theatre as his interests in the 1936 *Who's Who*; he and all the Downs Butchers, and Alwyn in earlier times, often travelled abroad together, as photographs show.

1 Carpenters' Company, Court Records and Inventories, 1919, 1926, 1933. Cited in letter 19 October 1999 from Archivist to Paul Hallam.

2 1933 Dover Town Council report on the Astors.

3 1920 *The Times*, 21 July.

4 'The Vacant Mess', *The Times* [London, England] 12 July 1924 9 p16, *The Times Digital Archives*. Web, 31 August 2016.

5 Ramsden Work Books: 1922, Q147; 1923, 148; 1924, R29, R 32; Undated order for fire screen with arms: 1924, R66, R80; 1925, R111.

6 Whitstable Parish Church Archives (All Saints) 1925, 1931.

7 DCb/EF/Faculties/Whitstable All Saints 7, 19 August 1937, Canterbury Cathedral Archives.

8 Walker Art Gallery, Liverpool, exhibition catalogues 1921–1938.

9 *The Dream Ship*, Ramsden's Special Order Workbook, 890.

10 May 1923, *The Times*, The Sir Percy Cox nef, Ramsden's workbook entry 1011.

11 BMD Marriage Certificate, 3 September 1927, Kensington

CHAPTER 8
Commissions for State and Church

As noted in the introduction, it was through the Cumberbatch trophy that I first developed an interest in Omar Ramsden. In 1931, my Great Aunt Alice Beatrice Martha Cumberbatch commissioned him to make a magnificent silver cup which was to be presented annually to the individual or company who made the greatest contribution to air safety in that year. Miss Cumberbatch lived in Ealing; a member of the nearby Hanworth Flying Club, she took her flying certificate there. She had already presented the Club with a Ramsden writing pad in 1926 and a paperweight earlier in 1931.[1]

The Opening of the Hanworth Flying Club in 1929.
(*Courtesy of the Honourable Company of Air Pilots*)

In the 1930s, commercial flight was very much in the developmental stage; Alice, as recorded in *The Aeroplane*, March 1932, wanted to recognise 'the reliability of the pilots who fly to and fro without necessarily breaking records or attempting long and arduous flights'. The design of the trophy incorporates the Desoutter monoplanes widely used at Hanworth, within a setting of clouds and flashes of lightning. Due to various difficulties the cup was not presented through GAPAN until four years later, in 1936. (GAPAN, the Guild of Air Pilots and Air Navigators, now renamed The Honourable Company of Air Pilots.) His Royal Highness The Duke of Kent, Grand Master of the Guild, made the first presentation at the Mansion House to Squadron Leader H. G. Brackley and a team from Imperial Airways. In 2015, it was presented by His Royal Highness The Duke of Edinburgh and has been awarded most years in between except during World War II.[2]

The journal *Flight* reported on the gift in 1932, adding that regulations for its future presentations were then being framed by the Hanworth Club in conjunction with the Royal Aero Club.[3] The writer added that the cup:

… was designed and executed by that well-known craftsman Omar Ramsden, whose house at St Dunstan's, Seymour Place, S.W.10 is one of the most attractive showrooms imaginable.

The presentation was also written up in *The Aeroplane*; the writer of the article added that, 'A Mr Omar Ramsden, who designed the Trophy, was persuaded to interpret it to the meeting.' He had been encouraged to make

THE DUKE OF KENT presenting the reliability trophy of the Guild of Air Pilots and Air Navigators to Squadron Leader H. G. Brackley at the Mansion House yesterday.

The Duke of Kent making the first presentation of the trophy in 1936. (*Courtesy of the Honourable Company of Air Pilots*)

a flight at Hanworth himself, in order to understand the experience and inspire the design.[4] He:

> explained how, when he had made his first flight, the machine had seemed to make tracks in the air and how the design of the trophy represented achievement after difficulties.

The Cumberbatch Trophy, 1931.
(*Courtesy of the Honourable Company of Air Pilots*)

As the donor of the trophy, Alice was later given the Freedom of the City of London. On 8 December 1960 she was 'made free in the Company of Air Pilots and Navigators' and also made an Honorary Life Member of the Guild.

Researcher Alison Hodgkinson, who has personal connections with the Guild, became intrigued by the story of the trophy, and wondered who the unknown Miss Cumberbatch might be. Her findings were published in the *Guild News*, and later in the *Guild of One-Name Studies* published by Bob Cumberbatch.[5] Purely by chance I came across the study, contacted Alison, and we exchanged information. She provided the information about the Guild and the history of the Ramsden trophy, I was able to tell her about the Cumberbatch family.

The photograph dated 1894 shows the Cumberbatch siblings: Alice as a small child, her sister Lily who became Gerald Downs Butcher's mother-in-law, and Percy, the author's grandfather, in their garden at Bradmore House in Hammersmith. This was then a house in a large, peaceful garden. After years of being used as a London Transport bus garage, it was partly restored, and is now a restaurant in the centre of a massively built up area.

The Cumberbatch Siblings, 1894.
(*Credit*)

Alice's own story is an interesting one, particularly the way in which the funding of the cup came about. While living in Ealing Alice wrote articles for the local paper, the *West Middlesex Gazette* expressing her strong opinions on all kinds of subjects. She became friendly with Mr Chambers, the editor, and he proposed marriage. It seems they were engaged for over twenty years, and he appears with her on many family photos, but Alice would never name the day, for fear of what marriage might entail.

After waiting all this time Mr Chambers had had enough; the story goes that Alice's niece Pamela (who later married Omar's stepson) saw him on the underground with 'another woman', and that was that. At all events he married someone else, following which Alice sued him successfully for breach of promise. Her family members were mortified, they would not have wished anyone to think she did it for financial gain. He had broken his promise to her, she had lost face by being jilted, she considered he should be punished. She was a strong-minded woman, not easily dissuaded from her intentions. Soon afterwards, Alice used the resulting funds to commission the cup from Omar Ramsden, then internationally renowned.

In 1931 Ramsden gave an interview to a Sheffield journalist following an exhibition. A contemporary cutting reports:

> Among the principal exhibits were a challenge cup of handwrought and chiselled silver for the Hanworth Flying Club, given by a woman donor to encourage reliability in aviation...Mr Ramsden told me it had taken him nine months to make the trophy for the Hanworth Club.... 'I take a long time over my work,' he said. 'I like to put a thing on the shelf when I am doing it, and think about it.'

Perhaps it was through Alice's commissions that the Cumberbatch family, Omar and the Downs Butchers got to know each other well and Alice's niece met and married Omar's stepson, Gerald Downs Butcher in 1933.

Many other Livery Companies and Guilds in the City of London have special silver designed by Ramsden. He had a reputation for creating an original and individual design appropriate to each one's role and history. Still in the partnership years, Ramsden and Carr had made the 'Pullman' Rosewater dish for the Worshipful Company of Leathersellers in 1913 and a Standing Salt for the Worshipful Company of Merchant Taylors in 1914; one of its decorative figures is 'St George the patron of England … to mark its having been made in the time of a great War'. A Loving Cup and Cover for the Worshipful Company of Dyers was also made in 1914; Ramsden wrote: '…the lid is surmounted by a swan, in allusion to the rights of this Company over the Swans of the River Thames'. Ramsden describes these works in the leaflet for their St Dunstan's exhibition of November/December that year.

The Fishmongers Company was presented with a silver gilt salt in 1927, known as the Nicholson Salt. Six fluted columns with flame finials enclose a kneeling figure of St Peter holding a net filled with the miraculous draught of fishes. Several letters and drawings are extant about the design and making of the salt.

The same year, 1927, William Edgar Horne commissioned 'The Horne Cup and Cover', which he presented to the Clothworkers Company in January 1928 to mark the 400th anniversary of their incorporation. The names of eight members of the Horne family, all former Masters, are engraved on it. The Company has notes from Ramsden in their archives, one describing the cup in detail: it was made of chiselled 18 carat gold, weighing 68.75 ounces troy, and

Ramsden's drawing of the Nicholson salt, c1893. (*Courtesy of Ralph Holt*)

valued at 500 guineas. The cup was obviously very well received; a note in Ramsden's hand dated 28 January 1928 thanks a Mr Evans for letting him know how well it was appreciated.[6]

Later in 1928 work began on one of Ramsden's most complex pieces, the Collar and Badge of the Honourable Company of Master Mariners, presented to them by Viscount Rothermere. Made of finely wrought 22-carat gold, jewelled and enamelled, the central badge can be separated from the collar, to be worn on less formal occasions. It bears the Coat of Arms of the Company, correctly coloured, and their motto. In front of this is a mermaid giving a handful of pearls to a merman. Surrounding this are seven diamonds representing the lights guiding mariners over the seven seas. The articulated collar shows sea figures amongst waves, seaweeds, coral, shells and fish. Work on the collar took several months, and a model of it was worn by the First Master, His Royal Highness The Prince of Wales (later His Majesty Edward VIII) when he presented the Company with their deed of incorporation. Omar was invited to meet the Prince of Wales in connection with the design; this was mentioned in the Court Circular in *The Times* of 28 May:

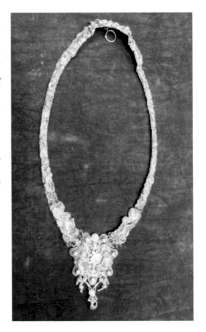

His Royal Highness subsequently received the Viscount Rothermere, Sir Burton Chadwick (Deputy Master of The Honourable Company of Master Mariners) Captain F. R. O'Sullivan, and Mr Omar Ramsden.

Ramsden kept the preliminary copper model, his widow presented it to Sheffield Museum after his death.

The collar and badge of the Honourable Company of Master Mariners, 1928.
(*Courtesy of the Honourable Company of Master Mariners*)

Another 1928 commission in June may have reminded Omar of his Sheffield days. He and two others designed a set of modern silverwork which the twelve Chief Livery Companies of the City of London wished to present to the Cutlers Company of Sheffield. As students in Sheffield, Alwyn and Omar competed for prizes from them, Alwyn had won an award.

In 1929 Ramsden's name appeared in the *University News section of Official Appointments and Notices* section of *The Times*, as the maker of 'a massive hand-wrought silver candelabra for St Salvator's Hall' in St Andrew's University. It seems that whenever an important presentation of his silver was made, his name was always mentioned with pride as an indication of quality.

The *Sheffield Independent* in 1932 recorded in *The Talk of London* notes that Her Majesty Queen Mary had just presented a sweetmeat dish to the Victoria & Albert Museum which she had bought about three years previously.[7] The following year the same section recorded Ramsden's work in the Suffolk Street Galleries, where the United Society of Artists was exhibiting:

Mr Omar Ramsden is represented by some exquisite work of which the most novel is an aspirin box in silver. In the old days people had their snuff boxes; today snuff has given way to aspirins...He produces new and lovely shapes in profusion and they are, I am afraid, often copied without acknowledgement... he knows that mass production can never give the same bloom that comes from the hand of the master craftsman. That is why he does not worry if unscrupulous manufacturers steal his ideas'.[8]

By the 1930s, Ramsden had developed an interest in mazers which had begun in the later 1920s, together with reviving the skill of making them.[9] He obviously spent a considerable time researching the subject and produced a descriptive booklet for private circulation, illustrated by photographs of several examples he had made. Essentially a mazer is a bowl made from maple wood, with a decorative band of a precious metal around the rim. He gave a historical account of its development from the thirteenth to the fifteenth century. He thought the word 'mazer' was probably from the Flemish and old English words, 'maserle' or maple wood, and 'maeser', an excrescence of the maple tree. He explained:

> ... all mazers, properly so-called, are of that twisted and mottled wood which is obtained from a certain kind of maple tree which bears many 'bols' or excrescences on its trunk. The speckled and grained effect of this wood, when turned into a bowl, has been explained as being due to the rapid boiling up of sap each springtime, in this particular tree.

The numbers of bols of this kind on a tree are necessarily limited, so were particularly valued for the making of characterful bowls. Each was turned, carefully cured – which might take up to a year – and hand polished to make a drinking vessel. After this treatment the bowl was ready for the addition of the integral band of silver or gold; as well as being highly decorative this gave height to a shallow bowl. A mazer might last hundreds of years. Each mazer being highly individual in form, the silver mounting had to be carefully designed in proportion to the bulk and colour of the wood, which required both practical skill and artistry.

A Mazer bowl, 1938. (*Private collection*)

Ramsden had found that this process was lost until 'recent research and experiment was made.' He does not say whether this was done by himself, but does mention that it was 'a matter requiring no little skill and knowledge, much patience and considerable time to accomplish'. He had the wood cured for between one and three years by Rogers & Co. of Oxford, in the High Street, then treated and finished in his own workshop.

The earliest mazers known at the time Omar was writing were two from the early fourteenth century, in the reign of Edward II. He noted that the earliest were wide and shallow, rather in the form of Greek libation bowls, but later ones became deeper and more cup-like, even with a circular foot. It seems that in Canterbury in 1328 there were 182 mazers; as he wrote, Ramsden knew of only sixty mediaeval examples in the country. He described the way in which the central part of the inside of the bowl was often decorated to hide the original marks of making, and how this developed into a 'boss' or 'print' which became a primarily decorative element.

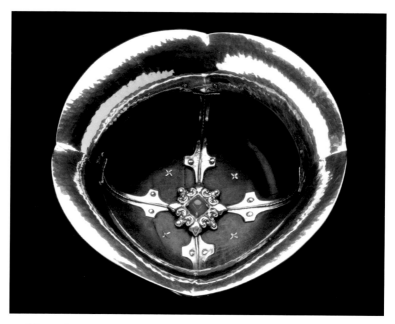

Mazer showing the decorative central boss, 1935. (*Private collection*)

As he created more mazers in the later 1920s and 30s they became a popular choice for presentation and ceremonial pieces for companies and individuals, where formerly a traditional purely silver bowl or cup might have been chosen. The Governor of the Bank of England received one in 1931, the Goldsmiths Company in 1932, the Ironmongers Company in 1936 and a handsome bowl was presented to Lord Middleton, Deputy Governor of Cable and Wireless (Holding) Limited in December 1936. In May 1937 another mazer was presented when Mr Ramsay MacDonald opened a large extension to the Paint Research Association; one of his duties was to unveil a bronze tablet made by Ramsden but designed by a Mrs Hinchley. One must assume Ramsden was sufficiently satisfied with someone else's design on this occasion to agree to execute the work.

Also in 1937, the Middle Temple acquired a mazer, often known as the *Three Kings Mazer*. In 1936 there had been three British kings, George V, who died in January, Edward VIII who reigned uncrowned until his abdication in December and George VI. Paintings of their crowned heads, together with Queen Mary's, decorated the rim of the bowl. The name of 'Three Kings' may also have been a reference to the late fifteenth-century mazer belonging to Corpus Christi College, Cambridge, which Ramsden would have known, though the Kings in that case were, by tradition, Melchior, Balthazar and Jasper.

Seals, medals and badges were a smaller but consistent part of the firm's output. *The Times* showed a medal for the Territorial Army Boxing Championships held in the Albert Hall in March 1932. Adjoining a photograph of the medal is wonderful sketch advertising a new Riley Alpine Six, the kind of new motor design which Ramsden was known to admire. The same year he made a silver gilt and enamel badge on a ribbon for the Mayor of Dover, Mr F. R. Powell, and a similar pendant on a chain for his wife. Both depict St Martin of Tours on horseback cutting his cloak in two and giving half to a beggar, in reference to the local St Martin's Priory. The badge and pendant are held in the Wilson Museum, Cheltenham. They were obviously admired as Ramsden was given another civic commission for Dover the following year. This was for two caskets of oak and silver to contain scrolls giving Freedom of the City of Dover to Major the Hon John J. Astor, MP for Dover from 1922 until 1948. His wife Lady Violet Mary Astor who was later to become the first woman MP received the same honour. The oak for the caskets was reputed to have come from HMS *Victory*. Ramsden is thought to have bought some of the oak and used it in several pieces, including the Noah's Ark for the Worshipful Company of Shipwrights.

In July 1932 came the opening of a new dry dock at Southampton by Her Majesty Queen Mary, widely reported and photographed by the press. This dock for the repair and maintenance of ships was then the largest in the world, big enough to take the huge ocean liners which were then the usual means of crossing the Atlantic. The Queen was presented with a libation bowl made by Ramsden, the two handles of this elegant bowl are formed by two female figures leaning backwards, with evident art deco influences.

Christmas card from Omar and Anne Ramsden to family in the USA, 1932.
(*Walt Ibbotson*)

In March 1933 Ramsden was commissioned to make the Master's Badge for the Worshipful Company of Carpenters 'to commemorate the 600th year of the making of their 'Boke of Ordinances' in 1333'. He had already made the memorial dish for the bereaved fathers of World War I and went on to make further pieces for the Company. He was among the guests when the Prince of Wales presented the badge, which was set with precious stones, the centre being enamelled with arms on white gold. *The Times* reported on the event and recorded that an 'amusing speech [by the Prince] to the Company was reported and an excellent dinner was enjoyed'. The advertisement adjoining this press report shows two ladies elegantly clad in ermine capes and evening dress, the 'latest Modes'. Above the badge is a photograph of Prime Minister Ramsey MacDonald meeting Signor Mussolini in Ostia.

In April 1938 Ramsden produced the wonderfully original Noah's Ark for the Worshipful Company of Shipwrights, which has pride of place in their ceremonies today; their motto is 'Within the Ark, Safe Forever'. Once again, the oak used for the base was said to be part of that from Nelson's HMS *Victory*. Like many of Ramsden's commissions for Guilds, it was marked as '*wrought … by command of* ', and in this case, Sir Charles Barrie MP to mark his year as Second Master to the Company. A donor presenting an expensive silver gift to his Company would no doubt rather like to follow the custom of having his own name inscribed on his gift. The house section of the ark, with a dove above the entrance, holds cigars and can be detached to hand around. The ark and boat are mounted in silver, and the whole is set on a sea of green wood, resting on an ebony plinth.

Another commission of 1938 was a silver cup for the Society of Apothecaries of London, a gift from the Bank of England to commemorate the eighteen years of service of the medical officer to the Bank. The base was decorated with six symbols of the arts of healing and of banking, and the knob of the lid was in the form of a bunch of herbs, again, an appropriate design reflecting the interests of the society.

Cigar holder in the form of Noah's Ark, 1938.
(*Courtesy of the Worshipful Company of Shipwrights*)

One of Ramsden's more unusual commissions of the 1930s was to construct a scale model in silver of the newly heightened and widened Aswan Dam on the River Nile. An accompanying book, *The King's Model of the Aswan Dam*, tells the story of the dam's construction from its beginning in 1898.[10] The Nile rose in Lake Victoria and flowed north for six hundred miles. Every year the river level rose in August, filled by rain and melting snow in Abyssinia. The Nile flooded its valley right to the edge of the desert, depositing the fertile silt which enabled Egypt's agriculture. This was Egypt's only reliable source of water, and for thousands of years it had been spread by irrigation. The proposed dam would be of huge benefit in allowing continuous control of the water.

In 1898 work was begun on the construction, with British engineers, thousands of Egyptian labourers and hundreds of skilled Italian masons. It was opened with great ceremony in December 1902 by King Edward VII's brother, His Royal Highness Prince Arthur of Connaught, (a Ramsden collector) and the Khedive.

Five years later it was thought desirable to heighten and widen the dam to increase its capacity, and construction began again in 1907. The opening ceremony was held in December 1912, when Lord Kitchener represented the British King George V.

By 1929 it was considered that a further extension would be beneficial and a second heightening was launched in January 1929. Sir John Norton Griffiths' British company won the contract. However, disputes arose between the Egyptian government and the company over the speed of the work and the skill of some of the Egyptian engineers and work came to a halt on 21 September. Sir John's suicide was reported on 27 September and construction was hugely delayed. At the end of 1930 the contract was re-assigned and the dam officially opened on 5 January 1939, by King Farouk I, who was to be the last King of Egypt and Sudan.

Presumably the scale model, 1/200, was commissioned quite early in the construction as it has Ramsden's mark for 1934. It measures just over 9 x 20 x 10 inches (23.8 x 52.7 x 26.4 cm) and is mounted on a wooden base. It includes accurate details of the original dam, the two additions to its height and the sluice gates. Ramsden must have had good access to drawings and models to produce so precise a scale

Model of the Aswan dam, opened by King Farouk I in 1939.
(*Courtesy of Ralph Holt*)

model, which would have required rather different skills from those needed for his more usual works. The Egyptian Royal Emblem is chased in the centre with an Arabic dedication in memory of the opening. As no one in the workshop would have been familiar with Arabic, it must have been written down for the chaser to carefully copy.

The model came to auction in Texas in 2014, but concern was expressed as to its authenticity; unlike every other piece Ramsden made, not all the separate constituent parts are hallmarked nor do they have his maker's sign. Though the work may have been started in 1934, if it was not finished until 1939, it has to be born in mind that Ramsden was often unwell in the year leading up to his death that year; his order books were not as well kept nor as detailed. It may be possible that this was how the hallmarking came to be overlooked.

Another important work of 1934 was made for presentation to Queen Mary, when in September she launched the largest ship ever made. Lord Aberconwy, Chairman of John Brown Shipbuilders of Clydeside, asked Ramsden to make a casket for the occasion. Unusually it was of hand-wrought and chiselled modern Staybrite steel, this being a brand name of a Sheffield company. Mounted in gold and silver gilt, it bore the Arms of the Queen and of the John Brown Company. The lid of the casket is modelled and chased with a liner on a turbulent sea, sailing to North America from the English Channel. In the north are Polar bears, icebergs and the Aurora Borealis, with dolphins and mermaids in the southern waters. The launch of the Cunard White Star express liner 534, named SS *Queen Mary*, was a sufficiently important occasion for the BBC to make one of their earliest outside broadcasts, which reached as far as India and the United States.

The following month of October Ramsden found himself listed in the '*Court and Social Arrangements for Today*'. This time it was not for a commissioned piece of work but for a lecture to the Goldsmiths Company. He was, by this time, highly sought-after as a speaker as well as an Artist Goldsmith. The talk was entitled *Mediterranean Digressions and Divagations* (the two words meaning much the same thing).

1935 took Ramsden away from his workshop and the lecture hall when he was invited to visit Iraq. This was to prepare for a commission for an oriental-style casket to be presented to King Ghazi of Iraq to commemorate the opening of a 600-mile pipeline to carry oil from the Kirkuk oilfields to the Mediterranean. This huge project was the result of co-operation between the Iraq Petroleum Company and the governments of Iraq, Trans-Jordan, Palestine, and the Syrian and Lebanese Republics, countries through which the pipeline was laid. British, French and American companies and governments all had interests in this major feat of engineering. The casket was made from ninety ounces of silver and ten ounces of gold, commensurate with the grandeur of the scheme. The events were fully reported in the British press.[11]

By 1938 the possibility of war was becoming ever more likely and in September British Prime Minister Neville Chamberlain made his infamous speech containing the well-known phrase, *Peace for our time*, often misquoted as *Peace in our time*. Possibly it was meant to be *Peace for a time*. Chamberlain had hoped that the Munich agreement he had just signed with Adolf Hitler would avert war. In the short time before war finally did break out in September 1939, a thankful donor commissioned a plate from Ramsden inscribed with the phrase above. The dish was brought to the Antiques Road Show by a member of the Chamberlain family and was highly valued, both for its historical interest and the fact that it was made by Ramsden.

Ecclesiastical commissions were another major part of Ramsden and Carr's work. Both were Artist Members of the Church Crafts League, which had been founded in 1899, at a meeting in Leighton House, as 'A Society Formed to Foster the Beautiful in Holy Places'. In their Fifteenth Annual Report of 1915 the members briefly re-stated their aims, which included 'that of educating public taste in the direction of our ideals. We have sought to do this by means of meetings, lectures and exhibitions'. Speakers included well known architects, critics, artists, bishops and other clergy, on a wide range of topics. The League compiled a directory of artists and crafts people with skills of the highest quality, which church authorities could freely consult when considering commissioning a work of art.[12]

Membership comprised artists in many fields; architects, metal-workers, needlewomen, embroiderers, sculptors, stained glass workers, wood workers, calligraphers, book binders, illustrators and others. Most were adherents to the principles of the Arts and Crafts movement and showed work in their exhibitions. For the craftsperson, membership of the League might bring work their way, certainly both Ramsden and Carr benefited. One had to apply for membership and provide examples of work, these were examined for a high standard of quality. The 1915 Annual Report showed that of the eight who applied for membership, only three secured election. From its 1899 beginnings to the 1915 report, the League had advised in about 1700 cases, around 400 churches had followed their guidance.

Networking amongst members was obviously helpful. In 1936, the Bishop of St Albans had been President of the League while Omar was Chairman. He was commissioned to make three memorial church wardens' staves in wrought silver and ebony, with figures of St Alban in chiselled silver gilt, for the cathedral in that city.

When shortage of funds hit the League in the depression years and at other times, it was recorded that the Artist Members were generous in making cash donations to keep it going. Omar was mentioned for his continuous generosity in the 1939/1940 Report which recorded his death.

Laurence Turner, who was tasked with executing Carr's gravestone according to his design, was their Honourable Treasurer for some years. He too had been a generous donor in the League's difficult times. Captain Carr's death was recorded as an Artist Member in the 1939/40 Report, but with no comment.

In a review of an exhibition of their work in January 1923 Ramsden showed 'a wide range of altar furniture in beautifully hammered silver'. This might be a processional cross, an altar cross and candlesticks, a monstrance, a chalice and paten, an alms dish or a pyx. Additionally, there was a continuing need for smaller medals and crosses, perhaps for new clerical appointments or translations.

OMAR RAMSDEN
Artist Goldsmith
London, England

Cross presented to Bishop Arthur Greaves when he was consecrated Suffragan Bishop of Grantham in 1935. (*Courtesy of Jane M. W. Campbell, University of St Andrew*)

Just before Christmas that year, on December 20, an ornate silver altar cross, 'the work of Mr Omar Ramsden,' was presented to Rochester Cathedral by Dean Storrs. At the other end of the social scale, the adjoining advertisement to the accompanying photograph in *The Times* shows a forlorn child in a Christmas charity appeal in the language of the period, '*The Waifs and Strays Society*'.

A very handsome processional Cross was gifted to Bath Abbey in 1925, by Mrs W. S. Shelton, in memory of her husband. Is it significant that Ramsden's name appears at the top of the explanatory brass plaque, above that of the donor? We do not know whether it was Ramsden who decided on the layout of the wording. Possibly he was so renowned at that time that someone else chose to put his name at the top. The central panel of the cross shows the Adoration of the Shepherds on one side and the Adoration of the Kings on the other. The cross is still used in the daily life of the Abbey, and can be seen in the nave.

Left: The Shelton processional cross in Bath Abbey, 1925. (*Photo by Alan Morley*)

Below: Detail of the Bath processional cross, depicting the Adoration of the Shepherds. (*Author's photo*)

The Roman Catholic Westminster Cathedral has several works from the partnership days displayed in the Treasury, including the magnificent early monstrance of 1906, considered to be one of their finest works. Margaret Stella Nickols commissioned the monstrance in thanksgiving for her vocation to the nuns of the Order of Poor Clare. There are enamelled figures of Saints Clare, Peter, Francis and Colette, and on the reverse four enamelled scenes from Christ's life. It seems possible that the enamelling was done by Carr, and the original design was probably prepared by him rather than Ramsden since he retained it on the dissolution of the partnership. As a devout Roman Catholic he would have had a particular interest in designing a monstrance, used for displaying the Eucharistic Host to the congregation. After Carr's death the design was given to the Cathedral by his brother and niece, to be kept with the monstrance, which was engraved with words translated as 'Omar Ramsden and Alwyn Carr made me with skill and as their own work'. The treasury also displays an enamel and silver pyx, or small box for holding communion wafers, dated 1910, and an ornate silver-gilt jewelled morse, or clasp for a Bishop's cloak, presented to Cardinal Hinsley.

The monstrance for Westminster Cathedral, considered one of the partnership's finest works, 1906. (*Author's photo*)

The *Catholic Herald* of 1 June 1929 related the early history of a crown of diamonds, pearls, emeralds and rubies, set in gold, which was enabled by gifts from parishioners:

> The crown, which is valued at about £2,500, it was explained by Mgr Canon Howlett ... was the result of a paragraph in a cathedral publication which suggested a gift ... for a new crown for the Processional Statue of Our Lady ... The gifts were immediately forthcoming and these were then set in a frame of 18 carat gold.

This was not the end of the story of the crown, however. In 1969 Cardinal Heenan led a move of those who considered that it was more in keeping with Christian values to sell the valuable crown and use the money to relieve the poor. The crown was sold for £6,600. A less valuable 'everyday crown' was made to adorn the statue and is now in the Treasury.

The fashioning of a heavy silver cross and candlesticks for the altar of Coventry Cathedral was another important commission. In 1937 a major restoration and refurbishment was carried out by the Friends of the Cathedral, removing some Victorian installations to reveal mediaeval features. The cross and candlesticks were given by the family and friends of the late Provost Morton.

The following summer of 1938 a major Festival of Arts was held within the cathedral. Several concerts were broadcast by the BBC, and an exhibition of decorative arts was held, including some fine ecclesiastical needlework, and silver and gold by Ramsden, who continued to be Chairman of the Church Crafts League. These were widely reviewed and admired in the local press.[13]

Little could they have known that less than three years later the beautifully restored Cathedral would be destroyed by a torrent of incendiary bombs in World War II. Fortunately, just before this occurred Arthur Longman made a detailed drawing of the chancel and Ramsden's cross and candlesticks can be seen on the High Altar.

On 14 November 1940, the destruction was wrought. On the night of the intense bombing Provost Richard Howard rushed to rescue the cross and candlesticks and the colours from the fire. The cathedral was destroyed by the Luftwaffe raid which lasted eleven hours, killed around 600 people and injured more than 1,000. The cross and candlesticks are very heavy, and the Provost and three fire guards did remarkably well to carry them out of danger. Thanks to them they can be seen today in the new cathedral, together with a silver pyx and candle snuffer made by Ramsden in 1938.

In 1937/8, Omar donated two fine chalices and patens to the newly built Anglican church of St Cecilia in Sheffield, in memory of his parents. The gift was mentioned in the local paper, *The Star*, together with a photograph of Omar:

ART GIFT TO CITY CHURCH – MEMORIAL TO MOTHER

A Sheffield silversmith of international fame, Mr Omar Ramsden, has presented sacred vessels to St Cecilia's Church, which is to be dedicated by the Bishop of Sheffield on Saturday. The vessels were made by Mr Ramsden himself and he has presented them in memory of his mother. In 1914 he was appointed by the Board of Education as an examiner of metal work, gold and silver work, and jewellery for the National Competition.

In his student days he had taken part in these competitions himself. The base of the larger of the two chalices is inscribed with a memorial to both parents:

IN MEMORIAM BENJAMIN WOOLHOUSE RAMSDEN ET NORAH UXORIS AD USUM ECCLESIAE ET PARECIAE S. CECILIAE PARSON CROSS SHEFFIELD PRIMAE IBI CONDITE INVT. SCULPT.DD FILIUS OMAR OCT.MCMXXXVII

(In Memory of Benjamin Woolhouse Ramsden and Norah his wife for the use of the church and parish of St Cecilia, Parson Cross, Sheffield, on its opening. Designed and made by Omar their son, October 1937.)

The smaller chalice is simple but beautiful, intended for weekday masses; the larger one for Sundays and special Feast days. Both were removed to the church of St Bernard of Clairvaux on the closure of St Cecilia's.

The chalices made by Ramsden in memory of his parents, gifted to St Cecilia's church, 1937. (*Author's photo*)

Westminster Abbey commissioned Ramsden on several occasions. Subscribers had raised £450 for alms dishes in memory of the late Bishop Ryle. A feature in *The Times* in November 1927 described how:

> A prominent feature in the decoration of the east end of Westminster Abbey on all great occasions of ceremony is the magnificent collection of gold plate which it is customary to arrange on the High Altar … Of modern plate by far the finest specimens are four great silver-gilt alms-dishes … the work of Omar Ramsden, who designed them to harmonise with the magnificent pieces of Restoration plate, whose makers are unfortunately unknown.

One of Ramsden's very last works, unfinished at his death in 1939, was a Processional Cross of Abyssinian Ivory for the Abbey. Unusually, the cross is formed from one large tusk of ivory donated by Prince Regent Haile Selassie of Abyssinia in July 1924 before he became Emperor. It is 81 inches long and 18 inches across the arms. Enamelled shields at the top of the shaft bear the arms of England, Queen Elizabeth I, St Edward the Confessor and the Dean at the time, Paul de Labillière. A shield bearing the lion of Abyssinia was added in 1941. The cross was used in the funeral services of Her Majesty Queen Elizabeth, the Queen Mother, and of Diana, Princess of Wales.

The cross made of Abbyssinian ivory, gifted by Prince Regent Haile Salassie to Westminster Abbey, 1939. (© *Dean and Chapter of Westminster*)

It is often displayed in the Treasury today with other Ramsden works, including four chalices with matching patens, the two pairs of alms dishes mentioned above, a morse based on the Westminster Cathedral model, a pyx and a mace.

Though Omar designed and began the cross, he died before it was completed. Laurence Turner finished the work, and it was dedicated during the War, on Whitsunday, 12 May 1940.

These few examples demonstrate what a wide variety of works Ramsden produced, ranging from his major public commissions for British and foreign Royalty, for wealthy Guilds and Livery Companies and for church bodies, to his many smaller works for domestic situations, including the smallest of caddy spoons and simple jewellery.

---

1 Order for Hanworth Cup, 6860, Book R, PC, Original Order in code, p248, Order 4077, with costs as finished Dec.8, 1931. Cup £210 gross, costs of making, £132 6s 8d. Goldsmiths Archive

2 GAPAN Journal, June 1936, p5.

3 *Flight*, 11 March 1932, p219

4 *The Aeroplane*, 9 March 1932, p428

5 *On the Trail of Miss Alice Cumberbatch*, Alison Hodgkinson, the GUILD NEWS, *Journal of The Guild of Air Pilots and Air Navigators*, Issue 103 July 1997. Reproduced here by kind permission of the Honourable Company of Air Pilots and Alison Hodgkinson. Reproduced again with permission in www.cumberbatch.org, Guild of One-Name Studies, by Bob Cumberbatch.

6 Note from Ramsden to Mr Evans, 28 January 1928.

7 *Sheffield Independent*, Saturday 9 April 1932.

8 *Sheffield Independent*, Friday 30 June 1933.

9 Booklet on Mazers written by Ramsden, 1930s. Copy in PHA.

10 *The King's Model of the Aswan Dam,* 1934, privately published.

11 *The Times*, 14 and 15 January 1935, Iraq pipeline opening.

12 The Church Crafts League Annual Reports, 1915, 1935, 1936, 1938, 1939–40. Copies in the PHA.

13 *Midland Daily Telegraph*, 1938, 77 *Coventry Standard*, 1938, 79

CHAPTER 9

The Craftsmen and the Workshop

Given the success of the business, both at the time of the partnership and after, it is not surprising that Ramsden and Carr required a significant workforce to help them fulfil their commissions and obligations. They employed several men in their workshop whom they trained to the highest levels in the various aspects of a silversmith's work. The quality of their work was crucial to the continuing success of the firm.

A young Leonard William Burt was apprenticed to them in 1916 and a copy of the indenture for his apprenticeship survives.[1] He was about thirteen and with his mother Florence's consent and 'of his own free will' he agreed to learn the art of silver and metal work for the duration of eight years, beginning on 12 January 1918. This was not being 'trained informally' as has been claimed. The document covers more than four closely-handwritten A4 sized sheets, and gives an interesting glimpse into the usual expectations of masters and apprentices at the time, which seem now to be pretty rigorous:

> … during which time the said apprentice his said masters faithfully shall serve, their secrets keep, their lawful commands gladly do. He shall do no damage to his said masters nor see it be done of others but that he shall give warning to his said masters of the same…he shall not play at cards, dice, tables or any unlawful games … he shall not haunt taverns nor Play Houses … But in all things as a faithful Apprentice he shall behave himself towards his said masters [until] … 12 o'clock noon on July 9th 1925.

Messrs Ramsden and Carr were to instruct and teach him properly. His mother had the obligation to find 'sufficient meat, drink, clothing, medical attendance, house room or lodging and all other necessaries,' but they agreed to pay him weekly, starting with 10/– in 1918 (50p) and rising to 22/– in 1925. (£1 10p) (Except that if he was absent from work for any cause whatsoever he would receive no payment.) He had to work from 8am to 6pm with one hour for dinner, Saturdays from 8am to 1pm.

Leonard and his mother agreed that he would attend art classes for drawing, geometry and modelling for three nights a week, applying

Part of the apprenticeship agreement between Ramsden and Carr and Leonard Burt in 1916. (*Source unknown, copy in PHA*)

himself and endeavouring to 'improve himself in knowledge in every possible way'. In consideration of the distance he would have to travel to those classes, he was to be allowed to leave work at 5.30pm on those days. 'Furthermore they agree to allow him to absent himself from their employ for two clear weeks each summer by way of relaxation and holiday'.

The agreement was properly signed and witnessed by Leonard, his mother, Omar, Alwyn and Omar's brother Horace, who must have been in the workshop at the time. Burt stayed on for over twenty years, until Ramsden's death in 1939, attaining a high level of skill.

Leslie Durbin also came to the workshop as an apprentice, in 1929, when he was about fourteen. He became an admired silversmith in his own right in the years after Omar's death. But Durbin's relationship with Ramsden was complex: whilst he was appreciative of the opportunity to learn a trade from one of its best masters his respect turned to resentment when Ramsden's enduring fame continued to overshadow Durbin's own reputation, long after his death.

Durbin had been recommended to Ramsden for an apprenticeship by Augustus Steward, head of the metalwork department at the Central School of Art and Design. No doubt he was a promising student and must have considered himself lucky. Durbin completed the apprenticeship and stayed on for a further two years as a journeyman, earning about £2 1s 3d a week, until he was awarded a full-time scholarship and left Ramsden's employment. After serving in World War II he became an acclaimed artist/goldsmith, working in partnership with Leonard Moss.

In 1950, John Farleigh recorded conversations with Durbin for a chapter about the latter's work in his book, *The Creative Craftsman*.[2] Although it is primarily about Durbin's own work, it is revealing about his ten years in Ramsden's workshop:

LD: Steward, the head of the department, said to me one day: 'I have a job for you with Omar Ramsden'. Steward knew Ramsden personally; and after I had been introduced to him, I was asked if I would become an apprentice in his Fulham workshop. He was an artist and a master- craftsman working as I hoped to do myself. He had his own studio workshop employing about fourteen assistants.

Leonard Moss, my present partner, was a silversmith in the same workshop during this period. Steward had placed him with Ramsden the year before I came, and when I joined Ramsden as an apprentice, he (Steward) asked Moss to look after me and give me a helping hand. This Moss did and has done ever since.

JF What of your experiences while you were with Ramsden?

LD: I feel I was extremely fortunate in having been apprenticed to him although, (much to my horror) I found I was signed on as a chaser and engraver when I had thought I was going to be a silversmith... on looking back I am very glad I had to do these things, for I feel it is terribly important that silversmiths should know this side of their job...I know now the training was invaluable...I remember I was given a great gold dish to chase for the Earl of Derby when I was in my fourth year.

Leslie Durbin appears grateful for the opportunity and his reports on the other men and their working conditions give valuable insight into the day-to-day running of the workshop. He described conditions in the Maxwell Road workshop in a letter to Paul Hallam in 1999:

There was no running water, 1 WC in the garden, an outside tap the only source. In the workshop was kept a bucket of water filled and emptied from the outside WC. Toilet paper was newspaper or a telephone reference book which provided a good supply. The only space heater in the workshop was a small solid fuel kitchen range with oven. Len Moss and I used to arrive early in the mornings to light it in order to warm the shop up. There had been no Electricity supply up to the year I started working there, i.e. 1929. Lighting was by gas only. The workshop was in the garden of the house. Omar Ramsden owned and rented out the house to a person unknown to any of us.

The conditions may appear antiquated and old-fashioned but Ramsden had been an apprentice too, and probably based his workshop model on his own experiences. He was, however, not a tyrannical boss and encouraged the artistic and professional development of his craftsmen. When Durbin asked for two weeks off to finish a competition cup he was making, a previously unheard of request, Ramsden allowed it, asking to see the finished cup. 'When I showed it to him, his only comment was, 'It's very modern, isn't it?'

Perhaps this rather enigmatic response piqued Durbin and he felt unappreciated. Ramsden also sent Durbin off to the British Museum – in his own time – on occasion to study a figure or animal to improve his drawing.

Given his experiences of seeing family members suffer the pain and distress of bankruptcy, Ramsden would have been very aware of the need to maintain a business-like approach if the workshop was to survive difficult times:

> LD If you remember there was a bad slump in 1929–30. Ramsden had called us together, saying somewhat ruefully that, in view of the situation, we should most likely be reduced to garage hands, but being reluctant to disband us, he would like to keep us on if we were willing to continue on a short-time basis. This we did, but we were hard hit financially.

In 1946, Durbin and Leonard Moss set up in business, with three assistants. Moss had had an 'orthodox' apprenticeship in the trade before he went to work for Ramsden, continuing to learn at the Central School at evening classes.

> LM: I soon realised how much more there was in silversmithing than I had learned as a mounter in the trade, where my job had given me no scope whatsoever...'

Surely this is an example of just the sort of limiting experience for a working craftsman that Ruskin and Morris had been decrying fifty years before? But, Moss had acquired a very high standard of hammering at the Central School, which was not always what Ramsden wanted:

> When I was working with Ramsden he would say: 'Look here, Moss, I can't sell this work because I can't convince people that it is handmade, it's too crisp and clean.' There you have the designer imposing a technique on the craftsman that he doesn't believe in.

More insights into the running of the workshop come from others who worked there too, including Ernie Wright who was a chaser and engraver and worked long term for Ramsden, and who taught Durbin valuable skills. His name was, in fact, Wilfred, but Ramsden considered that too formal and said that he was to be called Ernie, and so he was. Ernie related to Mark Gartrell, a silversmith practising today, who worked briefly as a student for Durbin, some anecdotes about life at Maxwell Road, where whistling was not permitted. Ernie told Mark that being 'tight', or very careful with money, Ramsden provided the very cheapest Lifebuoy soap for the men, which would be pared down to the smallest slither before it was replaced. When a light bulb went in a dark corridor, it would be a very long time before it was replaced. Meanwhile the men would hang threads from the ceiling so that Ramsden, who was tall, would feel strands of thread brushing unpleasantly against his face as he made his way down the corridor. But apparently he took it with good humour.

While Mark was at Durbin's in Rochester Place, Sir Owen Wansborough-Jones was a popular visitor, always remembered by the men as he gave them ten-shilling tips, a very generous sum for the time. Sir Owen was a keen collector of Ramsden and Carr's work. Durbin himself could be moody and difficult, perhaps coming from a shyness he could not easily overcome, but he had a successful career and in the 1950s and 1960s was probably the best-known silversmith in Britain.

A. E. Ulyett, like Ramsden and Carr, had attended classes at the Sheffield School of Art, though he was a few years younger than them. By 1907 he too had moved to London, where he shared a house with two men, one of whom had a sister Annie Evers with whom Ulyett lived for nearly twenty years, before marrying her in 1940. They lived in Chelsea, a twenty-minute walk along the King's Road to the Maxwell Road workshop. He became the key man in the workshop, managing the day to day affairs and is thought to have enjoyed the privilege of sharing Ramsden's own workroom and office. In his will of 1935 Ramsden left Ulyett a bequest of £200, to be given if Mrs Ramsden died before him. He left his silversmith and foreman Walter Andrews £100 under the same conditions. Perhaps rather unfortunately for them, Annie survived Omar and presumably Albert and Walter received nothing at all. It seems an unusual arrangement; one wonders why Omar could not have left them the bequests unconditionally. He left a total of £13,208, so it would not have affected Anne greatly. Would she have disapproved of these gifts to his long-serving workmen, (and Jeanne Étève and her own daughter Joan) or begrudged it to them? Did she give it to them anyway? We do not know, as in the end Anne did inherit all and the men were entitled to nothing.

Durbin's attitude to Ramsden is definitely equivocal; on occasion he implicitly acknowledged the value of an association with the master to further his own business, as shown in this advertisement in *The Times*:

Mrs Omar Ramsden has given full consent to Leslie Durbin, formerly apprenticed to Omar Ramsden, to carry on the tradition of her late husband's work.[3]

On several other occasions an envy of Ramsden's success appears to surface and he displayed a desire to play down Ramsden's role as an active craftsman. Although Durbin and Moss's partnership was successful in its own right, time and time again, for many years after Ramsden's death, Durbin would be asked for information about the great man. In 1997 an interested enquirer wrote to Durbin asking about Ramsden. Durbin politely declined to provide information, saying that he had 'talked to so many writers who want to know something about Omar Ramsden that I feel weary of the subject'.[4] No doubt, as a silversmith himself, he would have much preferred recognition and discussion of his own work, rather than primarily being of interest as merely a former employee of the more famous master. As time passed, his resentment must have grown, resulting in his derogatory comments in the 1973 catalogue.

It is worth remembering that by the time Leslie arrived Ramsden was fifty-six and his work had long been critically acclaimed, evident from the contemporary reviews already included. In the early days with Carr the two men would have worked together at designing and making. By the time Durbin arrived thirty years later the firm was a much larger enterprise employing several highly skilled men. It would be quite usual at that stage of Ramsden's life to be much less 'hands-on' than when he began in 1898. It was and is the norm within most houses, including the most eminent, to put the name of the firm on all pieces leaving a workshop, no matter which craftsmen had contributed to it.

Later, asked if Ramsden designed all the work that was made in his shop, Durbin appeared keen to diminish Ramsden's role: 'Sometimes an idea for a design was passed on from the client; he also had a draughtsman who carried out his suggestions, which were then submitted to the client'. Durbin admitted, 'Ramsden did, however, have the first say in everything, and he supervised all the work carried out thereafter'. Durbin's implication that design was primarily carried out by the client and the draughtsman since Ramsden could neither draw or design is surely specious. Ramsden would not have received the critical acclaim of the preceding thirty years had this been the case.

The following extract from the conversation throws some light on the continuing discussion regarding the degree to which Ramsden participated in the hands-on craft work in the workshop. It has to be borne in mind that these are the thoughts of one man only, an employee who was not necessarily impartial, and who would be anxious that his own talents were not overlooked.

LD: Ramsden himself was not an expert craftsman, but when he couldn't show me how a thing should be chased or carved, he sent me to the manager, A. E. Ulyett, and it was he who maintained the high standard of workmanship in this particular kind of work.

There is plenty of evidence to support the notion that it was Durbin's ambivalent attitude to Ramsden, imparted to many others in conversation, which did much to tarnish Ramsden's personal reputation as a skilled designer and craftsman. My own feeling is that he felt a mixture of admiration and envy for his employer. Throughout his lifetime Ramsden's work was admired, well reviewed and sought after. But on the publication of the catalogue in 1973 by Birmingham City Museum and Art Gallery mentioned in the introduction, his reputation was seriously disparaged. This matters because the claims have continued to be repeated as facts ever since, often verbatim. Happily, they do not appear to have had much influence on the appreciation of his work, or its desirability to collectors. I would argue that the primary source of these opinions must have been Dr Cannon-Brookes' conversations with Ramsden's employees, particularly Leslie Durbin, as he was so frequently asked about his time with Ramsden.

Authors of subsequent articles in, for example, *Apollo, Connoisseur Magazine, Antique Dealers and Collectors' Guide,* all thank Leslie Durbin for his conversations with them.[5] However, I have concluded that in no way could Durbin be considered a disinterested party, so that his comments should not have been accepted as they appear to have been, as unbiased facts. As noted, the ambivalence in Durbin's attitude to Ramsden is evident on several occasions. It evidently annoyed Durbin that all work during his own time in Ramsden's workshop bore only the famous mark, 'Omar Ramsden me fecit'. Perhaps he saw himself as a spokesman for all unacknowledged craftsmen. In the 1973 catalogue he annotated his own Ramsden pieces, loaned to the exhibition, with such comments as 'possibly made by Walter Andrews, with a provenance from Ramsden's workshop', and 'with a provenance from Ramsden's workshop but actual maker unknown.' He continued the grinding of his axe in the attribution of designs and patterns he lent to the exhibition; for example, a circular plaque of which he says: 'Designed by Ramsden and William Maggs and the repoussé work executed by Leslie Durbin'; others were 'probably modelled by A. E. Ulyett', or 'executed' by him. One feels he would not have described them in this way had Ramsden still been alive. Further, it was quite common for several different craftsmen to work on a complex piece, each in his own particular realm of expertise, perhaps repoussé work or engraving, this is evident from the workbooks.

Another unsubstantiated claim in the 1973 catalogue was that 'Ramsden's drawings were by repute very primitive'. Did this also come from Durbin as the man on hand in the workshop? Ramsden had frequently won local and national awards for drawing and design while at Sheffield School of Art, more so than Alwyn Carr; though both were considered outstanding students. Surely it is probable that after thirty years of practice, the usual procedure would be that following consultation with a client about a particular commission, Ramsden would begin by sketching out his preliminary ideas? These can be seen in his workbooks. After discussing them in detail with his skilled draughtsman, often William Maggs, they would be given to that draughtsman to carry out the very time consuming work of drawing up a final design to Ramsden's satisfaction. It is quite unreasonable to infer that this meant Ramsden was unable to draw. The Victoria & Albert Museum has several of his drawings in their collections which can be seen online. Museums Sheffield has a sketchbook from his early travels abroad.

In his article, 'Thoughts on Modern Silver', Ramsden gave his thoughts on giving an over-prescriptive drawing to a craftsman:

In fact some of the best pieces of pure 'silver shape' have been raised under the hammer with only a sketchy sort of guide on paper. The hammerman's mind should be free … to take advantage of such natural forms as grow under the hand of an intelligent workman who has not got his eye constantly on an elaborate drawing.

Many of Ramsden and Carr's craftsmen were just that kind of intelligent workman.

The 1973 catalogue was also very critical of Ramsden's first known commission, won as a student. This was for the Sheffield city mace, which was accused of 'beefy historicism'. The donor had given very precise stipulations regarding its decoration and symbolism, which the catalogue did not mention. Ramsden himself had commented on the limitations which might be placed on a commissioned piece required to fulfil a traditional role, a mace was such an example:

He had admitted already that he had been unable to escape from the traditional form of the mace, and they all knew that a teapot had very unescapable [sic] qualities.

The Keeper of Metalwork at the Victoria & Albert Museum in 1903 evidently did not share Dr Cannon-Brooke's views, as he acquired an electroplate copy of the mace for their collection.

The catalogue notes continued their criticism:

'What is virtually certain is that Omar Ramsden never participated in the actual execution of any of the pieces which bear his signature.'

This is a major claim, endlessly repeated, about works carried out over a forty-year period. No evidence is offered to support this and the inference is that it came from conversation with Durbin. To refute it with just one more instance; Ramsden's invitation to membership of the prestigious Art Workers Guild in 1903 would not have happened had he been unable to show the exacting committee members work of his own design and making. The same applied to his membership of The Church Crafts League, the Royal Miniaturist Society and other professional bodies. Some of his workbooks post 1920 – the only ones still extant – show the time he himself spent on different pieces, unsurprisingly this would have become less in later years than in his earliest days with Carr.

Ramsden was the leader of a skilled team. He was undoubtedly in charge and he went to the workshop every day. He was dedicated and hardworking, encouraging his men to work to the highest possible standard. In addition to the everyday routine, doubtless he enjoyed talking with clients, discussing possibilities for their individual commissions. He would have taken pride in the fact that members of the Royal family appreciated his work; both he and Carr had built their reputations from modest beginnings without a background of privilege. Together, Carr, Ramsden and all the talented men they employed over many years, created a body of work still admired today for its design and craftsmanship.

1 Indenture of Apprenticeship, between Leonard Burt, Ramsden and Carr, 1916. Copy in PHA.

2 *The Creative Craftsman*, chapter 5, pp75-86. John Farleigh, G. Bell and Sons ltd. London, 1950.

3 Letter from Leslie Durbin to private collector, 18 November 1997, unpublished.

4 *Apollo*, vol 75, 1961 p184 Eric Delieb; *Connoisseur*, April 1974 Peter Cannon Brookes; *Antique Dealers and Collectors Guide*, Jan 1998 pp44–46 Sara Rossi.

5 *Goldsmiths' Journal*, 'Thoughts on Modern Silver', January 1928, p12.

CHAPTER 10
Ramsden in His Own Words

It is somewhat unfortunate that the catalogue of 1973 came to define Ramsden's character and reputation. He was a colourful person who was able to convey his thoughts and ideas in both the written and spoken word. With success had come demands to know more about Ramsden the man and he had obliged by responding to requests for articles and for lectures. Supported by a talented team behind him in the workshop, he could afford to take up these invitations to speak about his art. He gave dozens of lectures and was a popular and lively speaker. One of his earliest talks was for the subscribers to the *Journal of the Royal Society of Arts*, on the work of silversmiths and goldsmiths.[1] This was in 1910, when he was thirty-seven, still in the time of the partnership with Carr, and gives a clear idea of his personal characteristics and way of presentation. He appeared enthusiastic, wordy, deeply committed to his subject, steeped in the history of silversmithing, unafraid of making polemical statements and fond of irony in attacking those of whom he did not approve.

Ramsden claimed to have felt 'considerable trepidation … from the natural shrinking of the artist from talking about his work in public' but it has to be said there was little sign of diffidence. His opening remarks, or 'little grumble', illustrated some of his ideas and give a sense of the man himself:

> It is very unfortunate that the vulgar value of the silver and gold as bullion has always been a great drawback to the artistic appreciation of the craft … we come across the tendency to vulgarise the real value of the article by an exaggeration of its mere money value in weight and size.

He was critical of the system of hall-marking and considered that the hallmark:

> … has been a perfect godsend to a mass of experts and authorities created by it whose particular genius is compilation. These important gentlemen, with their magnifying glasses and much impressive antiquarian chatter… [mean that] it has become a question not of the art of the silversmith but the glorifying of the assay mark coupled, may I add, with that of the authoritative expert. The public is acquiescent, because it is so much easier to use tables than brains, and a band of auctioneers keep things going merrily.

Perhaps he never forgave or forgot his acrimonious correspondence over the mace with the Sheffield Assay Office in 1898.

He went on to describe, in graphic terms, the making of precious metalwork through various periods of history from the Romans in Carthage to the 'sad debacle of the Victorian time'. His love for fine works came through very clearly. His appreciation of the beauty of 'Catholic ritual, perhaps the richest pageant ever devised by man', is undeniable. His description of the 'gorgeousness' of a Catholic High Mass certainly shows his reverence for the atmosphere which beauty and ritual can evoke:

> Silver-sheathed high altar weighed down by golden crucifix and the six great candles of High Mass … the gold sobered by age, and the ever wreathing pungent-smelling incense, through whose curling clouds flash out their encrusted jewels, whose fire no age can dim, and before which progresses the ever shifting pageant of Roman Ceremonial, with all its lovely use of chalice, pyx, and gold encrusted tabernacle, monstrance and mitre of jewelled gold, bell and book, cross and crozier of lustrous silver, and cope and chasuble of cloth of gold, while around stand red-robed acolytes with standards of silver, bearing lighted candles, which sway over the heads of officiating clergy.

It has been said that he was a Roman Catholic but there is not much evidence to support this. He did not marry in a Roman Catholic church. He was happy to donate works to the Anglican Church in Sheffield in memory of his parents and was also happy to have this reported in the local press. Furthermore, after his death, his body was cremated, apparently in accord with his wishes, although cremation was not then condoned by the Roman Catholic Church. In 1910, he referred to the Eucharist as 'the symbolic body of Our Lord', whereas in the Roman Catholic view the bread actually becomes the Body of Christ at the moment of consecration. It is therefore more likely that his admiration for the Catholic Church was based purely on its aesthetics and his appreciation for good design and artistry, rather than anything more spiritual.

His talk moved on to technical matters: he disparaged the casting of silver, considering that 'the true silversmith today, as in the best Gothic times, is a beater of metals.' The famous Benvenuto Cellini came in for criticism, as he often would in Ramsden's later lectures and papers. He says of the year of Cellini's birth, 1500:

> To my mind it is the beginning of the decadence of the silversmith... [Cellini] was a great craftsman, and a great artist, no doubt, but his art was always that of a sculptor, working in precious metals by chance.

Of Cellini's most famous and admired work, the salt cellar (see page 199) he made for Francis I, he pronounced that this:

> zoological and aquatic Noah's Ark was as well packed as possible, and thoroughly represented its bizarre and bombastic author!

In a talk several years later he said again that it was a great disappointment to him:

> The greatest shock I ever had was when I was at last face to face with the silver and gold work of Benvenuto Cellini in Florence and Rome. Salt cellars so covered with squirming figures that one could not find

Cellini's masterpiece, the salt cellar made for Francis I in 1543.
(*Kunsthistorisches Museum, Vienna*)

the place for the salt. [He was] left cold by the much vaunted works
of the Italian Renaissance, as applied to silver, for Northern peoples.

The saliera, or salt-cellar is now in the Kunst Historisches Museum
in Vienna. The texts of his talks make fascinating reading, the open
discussions afterwards show that many disagreed with him on a variety
of topics, but his strong arguments and the passionate rendition of his
opinions must have made him a compelling speaker.

In addition to lectures and talks, he wrote many articles; his views on
his subject were frequently sought. During one particularly busy year,
1928, he contributed an article to the *Goldsmiths' Journal* in each of the
first four months, gave a major lecture to members in March, wrote
another article in June and delivered one more lecture in November
for the Royal Society of Arts. Together these '*Thoughts on Modern Silver*'

were billed as: 'an important series of articles specially written for the *Goldsmiths' Journal* by one of the leading artist-craftsmen of the day'.[2] These articles and lectures, possibly above all others, give a vivid and valuable insight into Ramsden the man and his beliefs.

He often began with high-flown rhetoric; in his January article, his opening paragraphs included a quotation from 'Omar Khayyam' and a comparison of the silver industry with the 'Sleeping Beauty', as having been dormant for about a hundred years. Happily, he did not continue in this elaborate fashion but moved on to his main themes. The first of these was the pitfall of re-hashing older styles of design, even though that:

> is a course that saves the designer's fee and has made much money in the past. [for manufacturers] ...It cannot go on much longer! Every time a die is re-cut or an old model used over again a little of its original sparkle and beauty is lost... No wonder France, ever in revolt, gave us the 'new art' of 1900 and the 'cube art' of 1925; products of sheer boredom.

His thoughts on 'those hammer marks!' were given, he clearly delineated his views on machine versus hand making, which are frequently misunderstood.

> The modern school of aesthetes, which began with William Morris and ended with Walter Crane ... gradually made a cult of hammer-marks as a sure sign of hand work. Like all cults it was pushed too far until the extreme 'arty thought' of today will maintain that hand work, however poor, is better than machine work, however good, and that hammer marks are a virtue in themselves... Let us make a firm stand and boldly say that hand work is futile unless it turns out better work than the machine... Also that hammer marks are a means to an end, not an end in themselves.

He moved on to 'Arty Pitfalls', such as the desirability of neatness.

> Personally, I dislike a perfect circle or a really straight line. The

Greeks understood this when they provided an 'entasis' or bulge to their apparently straight columns. Handwork should have freedom and show the living joy of the craftsman; the machine must be neat and accurate or it is useless.

Poor enamelling came in for his opprobrium:

Enamel properly employed is a glorious thing. Slopped over everything … as it was some years ago, it is nauseous! The rage for blobs of greeny-blue enamel, a decade ago, has almost killed what was a very interesting revival of a beautiful art.

On training in skills, he said:

I firmly believe that a successful silver designer should have 'been through the shops'… and should be able to do such work as a workman might jib at as being out of his experience.

It has been well-documented that both he and Alwyn had spent years in Sheffield learning the skills of their trade.

We have already seen how he would explain and discuss his own design ideas in detail with his draughtsman, usually William Maggs or A. E. Ulyett. Both had the skill to produce detailed working drawings, such a time-consuming task that it often made sense for Ramsden to delegate it to a competent man. The workbook entry for the Four Seasons Casket shows that Ulyett spent thirty-three and a half hours on the drawing, in addition to Ramsden's own time spent on design and supervision. The piece would then be crafted by one or several men, closely overseen by Ramsden.

In his talk, a photograph of a boating cup for Cambridge University illustrated this point: as 'an example of direct raising from the flat with only a slight sketch as a working drawing. Also showing what can be done by a very limited amount of ornament'. This was another aspect of design he advocated, so that the shimmering beauty of plain silver as a background to decoration could be appreciated.

All illustrations within the article were of his own work. As he saw this first article of four as preliminary 'destructive criticism', he felt 'it would be in poor taste to employ examples of other artists' work to illustrate remarks…'

The February article began with a host of metaphors and similes, this time he compared the silver industry with a 'ship at the mercy of the winds and tides…' As a luxury trade he saw the influence of 'the tide of fashion, especially as Woman, in all that appertains to luxury, is the real arbiter of purchase'. He made no apology for 'keeping a shop', recalling greats such as Donatello, whose name is undying, who also kept 'his little shop in Florence':

> Everyone who sells anything, be it brains in the Law Courts, silver in the High Street…keeps a shop, and there is nothing to be ashamed of in so doing. Business is the romance of modern times…

Once again the Victorian age came under fire but with an exception:

> … the Pre-Raphaelite epoch with all its lovely and delicate suggestions to the designer, of which the Arts and Crafts movement was an offshoot due to the genius and force of William Morris … its lasting and present representative is the small band of artist-craftsmen on the one hand and the 'arty' emporium on the other … it was a valiant effort and it is deplorable that its title should have been misappropriated and discredited by amateur and charity shows and societies … In its time it was a wonderful, beautiful and inspiring thing … On the general trade it had nothing like the effect that was expected.

He wrote of Morris's influence in the setting up of Guilds for art workers. Was he thinking of C. R. Ashbee's Guild of Handicrafts when he wrote about:

…the politico-socialistic idea of co-operative direction … which turned out to be useless meddling and mis-direction … the idea might work out well enough in a soap factory, but where every piece made was a fresh and different job, the cost of direction and book-keeping became a fatal handicap … the sole idea of an artist-craftsman should be to turn out unique and splendid pieces of rare beauty that will be a joy to possess. The spiritual exaltation of creative effort will be his principal reward.

The article covered themes he felt most strongly about: the poverty of design in silverware in England since the mid-nineteenth century, following the move to mass manufacture by an owner 'who is usually without the art education necessary to its proper use'. Next came the folly of copying older work, although:

In the pursuit of food and raiment I have myself been guilty of a few copies, from which I have gained much knowledge and much appreciation of the work of former goldsmiths… I hasten to add, however, that…I have felt it honest to add some little new touch here and there and a feeling of my own rather than produce a shame [sic] antique.

The March article argued that:

It would be quite reasonable to demand an explanation of what is meant by grasping at the spirit of old work instead of merely copying its outward forms … an extensive study of art-forms, as applied to precious metals has brought me to the fact that there are only two schools of art-thought… Northern and Southern.

He explained at length the difference he perceived between the art of 'The North', with the 'mysterious and subtle charm of all Northern handiwork', and 'The South'. His opinions were well argued and must have been the result of much thought, close observation and study. The careful reading of these articles gives a direct understanding of his views, rather than our having to rely on opinions attributed to him by others.

He did admit that there were in practice many charming transitional pieces between north and south:

In fact, as a holiday task, I once took great delight in designing an oak cupboard for my own studio, which had pierced Gothic panels and mediaeval mouldings blended with carved Renaissance pillars and a classic plan. Although this was by way of an experimental and costly toy, it still gives me pleasure to look upon.

The last article in the series centred on accepting that machine-made silverware was here to stay and that it would be best if manufacturers and artist craftsmen could co-operate and meet on equal terms:

The manufacturer … must no longer expect to buy art-forms and ideas at the same rate as he buys raw materials…The old idea of engaging an artist at a tempting and comparatively large salary to work in a factory has been tried out. It will never work because if the man is really an artist he cannot endure the suggestions and orders from manager and traveller… [Britain should aim to] obtain the fame of a world art-centre in the same way as the sound reputation of London as a centre of banking brings other business in its wake.

Ramsden maintained that using true artist-craftsmen would bring the standard of modern British silver up to that of foreign competitors, whose work was far superior at that time.

He did not admire modernism in any form:

Such passing phases as the present 'Cubist-futurism' so rampant in France, are really only novelties. As such they will have their day and as such they have been avoided by the cleverest brains on the Continent itself.

The March lecture at Goldsmiths' Hall was on Some Aspects of Modern Silver, with slides, followed by discussion.[3] The chairman opened by reminding members of the Company that the aim of the talk was to improve design and craftsmanship in silverware. Ramsden started with an assumption of diffidence, much like his 1910 lecture, not borne out in his talk:

> I would ask you to be kind and forbearing, and to put up with any little difficulties I may have in expressing myself as I should like to.

It did not take long for him to get into his stride however and pick up on his 'favourite' subjects. He expressed admiration for the medieval Goldsmith who:

> …in time became the Victorian manufacturer of silver plate, whose lack of foresight and headlong recklessness in the quest of profit has very largely brought us to the present position of over-production of commonplace goods…

He showed several dozen slides, discriminating and illustrating differences between the good and the bad; the early or modern; the very beautiful and the 'exceedingly ugly'; the 'very interesting' and 'very jolly' and the 'good, neat, uninteresting but well made'. His ideas on contemporary design were presented with force and conviction and he stated that he had 'no private axe to grind' but that his suggestions are for 'the younger men who come after'. He was then about fifty-five years old.

St Dunstan, patron saint of gold and silversmiths, was mentioned again 'whose statue you probably saw coming up the stairs – I wish it were a better statue, but there it is!'

He criticised many aspects of the silver trade; silversmiths' and jewellers' shop windows, competitions for silverwork designs, most of the silver cups given as prizes, including the English Football Association Cup. 'Could anything be worse? It seems to me to be the absolute limit of ugliness'. He praised the technical skills of the modern workman, the very beautiful glass now being produced in Czecho-Slovakia, and much of the handmade silver of former times. In modern times he considered that the best modern craftsmanship was that produced on the Continent.

It is in this talk that he expresses his views on machinery:

I am not one of those high art craftsmen who condemn machinery. For mass productions of good work for slender purses we must use it. It belongs to our time and I am no ostrich and do not wish to bury my head in the sands of yesteryear.

He refrains from naming the makers of any pieces illustrated, as 'smart and witty remarks of one artist on the work of his brother-brush, are much to be deprecated'. In spite of this he showed a slide of a German exhibit; the journal reported him as saying:

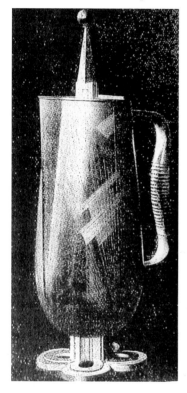

The silver jug made by the German instructor, C. Müller of Halle, described as a 'comic coffee pot' by Ramsden, c1928. (*Illustrated in the Journal of the RSA in Nov 1928*)

I call it a comic coffee-pot, with a weather signal on the top and some sort of weather chart on the side. I do not quite understand it. I would like to show it as an example of what not to do.

In the discussion following the paper, it had been praised by one speaker, but Ramsden questioned that opinion, saying: 'How a teacher could praise that coffee pot is beyond me. (Applause)' His was obviously the majority view.

Following the report of the talk in the *Goldsmiths Journal*, the editor received a letter from the maker of the pot, a Trade School Instructor at a German Industrial Art School. He pointed out that it was a wine jug, not a coffee pot, and said that he was 'naturally interested in the English criticism, and perhaps the occasion can be made for a mutual exchange of opinions and intentions'. The letter was politely restrained, given the diverse opinions expressed in it.

Ramsden's arguments for the improvement of the trade certainly sounded lively and engaging. The discussion was then opened to the floor; unsurprisingly, not everyone agreed with his polemical views. A Mr Harrison expressed the hope that silversmithing would not 'turn into a miserable affair like Art Nouveau. That to me is the sunken rock upon which the whole thing would be wrecked'. Ramsden replied that 'We must avoid, in our search for new good stuff, anything like the new art, or cubism, or futurism, because the public are not fools'.

He concluded that if his aims of improving design and marketing were to be fulfilled, it would be necessary to hold large and extensive exhibitions. The remark was picked up and developed later in an article by the Canadian National Exhibition. The whole text is an excellent exposition of many of his thoughts on the silver trade, after about forty years involvement in it.

His opinions continued to be sought. In the following month of June 1928 came an invitation to him and two other speakers to express their opinions freely in the *Goldsmiths' Journal* on the design of a modern ciborium. Essentially, all agreed that although great skill in technique was displayed, the design was over ornate and unsatisfactory, in spite of its monetary value of three thousand guineas. 'This is a clear case of executive skill outrunning creative faculty. Technique has got clean out of control'.[4]

Despite this conclusion Ramsden was nevertheless able to give a little encouragement to its unfortunate designer: 'With all its faults it is extremely interesting. Had it not been I should not have burned midnight electric light in order to give it careful and detailed consideration'.

Ramsden's last lecture for this very busy year was in November, on *English Silver and its Future*.[5] It was fully reported in the *Journal of the Royal Society of Arts* (The Royal Society for the Encouragement of Arts, Manufactures and Commerce) and *The Burlington Magazine*. His themes were, as often, the history of the art of silversmithing, ranging from 'the brawny men of sword and club', through classical art, to early Irish art and Saxon art. He digressed slightly here to mention St Dunstan, Patron Saint of Goldsmiths once more:

> That powerful Guild which guides and controls the silver production of England still has a somewhat foolish, gilt, wooden statue of him, taken from their 18th century State Barge, standing in their splendid Hall.

After St Dunstan he moved to the members of Medieval Guilds, whose 'restrictions enabled them to keep their work fine in quality and their members honest in their dealings...' Then came the Renaissance, which: 'As applied to craftsmanship, was but a stilted catalogue of festoons, urns, masks, fluted columns and the like, all very foreign to our national Art feeling'.

Benvenuto Cellini continued to be one of his bêtes-noirs, 'artist-goldsmith, sculptor, swashbuckler, author, genius and rogue, may be taken as a type of his age'. Ramsden was sometimes referred to as the Cellini of his age, probably those who wrote it had not read Ramsden's opinion of him, expressed more than once.

When he moved on to the Victorian age he gave his view of the low quality of the design and making of factory produced silverware as he had done many times before. This time he was highly critical of the Great Exhibition of 1851:

> As a callow youth I was given a ponderous book – '*The Illustrated Catalogue of the Great Exhibition of 1851*'. I hope most of you have never seen it as it is the most terrible and self-satisfied indictment that ever a nation produced against itself in the Court of art. [He excepted] the sturdy effort of William Morris, whose ideas, leading to the arts and crafts movement, have profoundly affected the present-day world of applied art. And his work goes marching on.

The talk demonstrated many of Ramsden's characteristics; he was well informed on the history of his art, he was passionate about upholding quality, he was enthusiastic, unafraid to be controversial. It is not surprising that he was sought after as a speaker. A lengthy and detailed discussion followed and Ramsden was given 'a most cordial vote of thanks.'

By 1934, Ramsden was still in demand as a speaker, his opinion being valued on all aspects of silver making and he was invited to give another lecture at Goldsmiths' Hall on *The Design and Application of the Plastic Arts to Gold and Silver*. The Chairman was the Director of Art Education in Birmingham, his opening remarks spoke of the eminence of the lecturers. (there were two that evening).

Ramsden's tone and language in this lecture is less provocative than in any previous talk mentioned. Coming six years after the last one outlined, perhaps he had mellowed a little. He said himself, 'As far as I can see, there is nothing controversial in our subject, because it deals with the origin of new designs or patterns'.

Familiar themes were touched on, 'A work of art should be judged by its innate beauty and function, not by auction room values, dates, and rarity'. A few incidental but interesting points from the lecture show again the character of the man. As usual he began with a historical background, he considered that the Mycaenae civilisation of *c*.3000 years ago was 'the golden age for repoussé work'. He drew an analogy between present day attitudes in the silversmithing trade and that of the Greeks of the later fifth century who were always disunited, 'so that when a highly organised individual like Philip of Macedon came along, he just wiped up the lot…' He had recently seen originals in a visit to Athens, and 'was startled by them. They were so extraordinarily modern…' When it came to modernity, he said that:

> Some motor cars strike me as being the most beautiful things our time has produced. Their lines are so beautiful; they suggest speed. The motor car is perhaps the most typical thing of our age.

Photographs showing him sitting in his elegant chauffeur-driven car with the Downs Butchers in the 1920s confirm not only his wealth but his love of good design.

On the profession of archaeology:

My own personal feeling is that we take a great deal upon ourselves when we dig up a gentleman who may have been buried some thousands of years. I do not think we have any right to dig him up, but it has become quite a profession.

He made yet another reference to Cellini, always a butt of his humour, saying he:

… is generally considered the greatest goldsmith of all time, largely founded upon his opinion of himself in his wonderfully entertaining memoirs.

Ramsden discriminated between Cellini's strong points and his weaknesses as he saw them. He had always admired Cellini's bronze statue of Perseus in Florence, 'but when it comes to silver and gold he seems to go quite mad'. Ramsden showed a slide of Cellini's famous salt cellar, and his own droll sense of humour:

It might suggest at first a representation of mixed bathing. It is of wonderful execution but, to my thinking, quite mad in design.

Another of the slides he showed was:

… an American example of René Lalique…. You see how terribly old fashioned the new things of thirty years or so ago are. René Lalique is an extraordinarily clever man, and what I show you is considered the best he could do at that time. Now it is extraordinarily old-fashioned looking. The next is Swedish…I find it very charming. It is avowedly quaint and childlike, there is a fine idea of proportion and it strikes me as being unpretentious.

His admiration of the Swedish work is in keeping with his stated preference for 'Northern' art for northern peoples.

Within this lecture Ramsden attempted the elusive definition of those qualities which elevated a competent work of craftsmanship into a work of art; as he put it, '"Art", with a capital A and in quotation marks':

> One may perhaps divide it into two parts, which, however, are inter-dependent the one upon the other – the emotional art of original expression, and the art of feeling which comes of sympathetic feeling. Very little of either of these qualities is present in any copy. [Art] cannot exist without fine proportions, composition, line, and judicious placing of design elements, but none of these, nor even all of them, will necessarily give you a work of art.

He was a man of his own time, moving design from the Victorian age into the twentieth century. Unlike some of his contemporaries in the wider world of art he had little interest in or admiration for anything 'modern', though Modernism was well established in the fields of painting, sculpture and literature by 1934. I would encourage anyone wanting to get a fuller picture of Ramsden the man to revisit the transcripts of these talks; they really do give a wonderful insight into his principles and his character.

---

1 *Goldsmiths' Journal*, 1910.

2 *Goldsmiths' Journal*, 'Thoughts on Modern Silver', Jan, Feb, March, April, 1928.

3 *Some Aspects of Modern Silver*, lecture and discussion at Goldsmiths' Hall, 8 March 1928. The Goldsmiths Company, Report of Lecture by Mr Omar Ramsden. Text typescript by Miss Eva Kyle, Goldsmiths' Library, File n.1.2 (1) mss no 5123. Reported in their journal, April 1928.

4 Points of View on a Modern Ciborium, *Goldsmiths' Journal*, June 1928, pp374-378.

5 English Silver and its Future, *Journal of the RSA*, vol 77, pp 51-71, 30 November 1928 and reported in *The Burlington Magazine*, July 1929.

CHAPTER 11

Ramsden's Connections with the USA and Canada

Ramsden had always had connections with North America; he had spent several years there as a young child, his father had returned and disappeared there after his business failure. His mother's close sister Elizabeth and her many children and descendants lived there, and later both his brothers, Wallace and Horace, settled there permanently with their wives.

Wallace had been born there, but was brought back to England as an infant; his first return visit to the USA was in 1903 on the *Ivernia*, as a young man. He was probably sent by the family to see his father Benjamin, but he did not succeed in bringing him back to England. Back in Sheffield, in 1910 Wallace married Beatrice Edwards; he was working as a silversmith and 'art worker', though later they set up a fruiterers' shop, perhaps for Beatrice to run. A daughter, Mamie, was born and the three lived in Sheffield with Norah, the boys' mother.

The youngest of the three Ramsden brothers, Horace, had continued living with his mother in School Road, Crookes, when Benjamin returned to the United States after his bankruptcy. Further up that road, Alice Wilshaw, always called Dolly, was working as an assistant in a draper's shop. Maybe Horace found excuses to call into the shop to talk to her, but however they met, they married in 1912, though there were to be no children of the marriage. Horace seems to have been the only one of the three brothers to serve in World War I. I can find no record of Wallace serving, although he was only thirty-two when the war started and might have been expected to be called up. He was reputed in the family to have delicate lungs and his eventual death was caused by pulmonary oedema which may be the reason he was not required to serve. It appears as if Horace joined under the Military Services Act of 1916, which brought conscription to Britain to replace the enormous losses of regular soldiers on the Western Front. It applied at first to all men between eighteen and forty-one, later increased to fifty-one. At first married men were excused compulsory service but this was soon amended and Horace was probably conscripted. He and Dolly were living in Putney then, not too far from Omar. The brothers obviously kept in touch, as in 1917 Horace was a witness to the signing of Leonard Burt's indentures on his apprenticeship to Omar and Alwyn. Possibly he did some kind of work for Omar. He described himself on occasion as 'artist', so may have had some useful skills. When he joined the army, aged thirty-one, his trade was given as Motor Driver and he was enlisted as a Mechanical Transport Learner in the Royal Army Service Corps.[1]

The thought of a life in the USA must have appealed to Horace as he and Dolly decided to migrate there permanently. In 1923, they sailed in Cunard's SS *Berengaria* from Southampton to New York where he planned to make a new life following his trade as a signwriter.[2] They went at first to Meriden and stayed with one of the many Ibbotson cousins, Robert. We don't know if his father Benjamin was still there or even whether he was alive.

Perhaps it was the economic slump and the widespread decline of so many businesses that caused them to move west to Los Angeles where they settled for good. Horace carried out various kinds of signwriting, particularly the lettering in gold paint required for offices of doctors, lawyers and others. After living there for five years, in January 1928 he and Dolly filed a notice of intention to seek naturalisation. Both had to swear that they were neither anarchists nor polygamists and did not support those practices. They renounced forever 'all allegiance and fidelity to any foreign prince, potentate, state or sovereignty, and particularly to King George V', of whom they were at present subjects. In 1930 American Citizenship was granted to them; they were then renting a home at 4660 1/4 Hollywood Boulevard for $50 monthly, the highest rental in the street.[3] It seems quaint now that the census of that year asked if people owned a radio, (they did). Ten years later, their circumstances much improved, they owned a home of their own in Glen Felix Boulevard, LA, valued at $2000. Horace seems to have retired in his fifties, with 'another source of income'.[4] Like both of his brothers, he died in his early sixties, while Dolly lived for another forty years to the age of ninety-nine.

Just before their grant of citizenship, in May 1928 they sailed to England for a long visit to Sheffield to visit Wallace, Beatrice, Mamie and Norah.[5] They must have talked enthusiastically about the opportunities in California as in May 1929 Wallace too emigrated with his wife and daughter on Cunard's steamship *Laconia*, leaving Norah in Sheffield.[6]

They settled permanently in the United States, living at first with Horace and Dolly on Hollywood Boulevard. Unfortunately, only six weeks after they left, Norah died on 3 July. Wallace and his family had lived with her for many years, the other two brothers having long since departed. Doubtless they had thought carefully about leaving her, taking her only grandchild with them, but go they did. Perhaps they had been affected by the current major recession and were finding it difficult to make a living. After Norah's death, probate was soon granted to Omar, but then revoked, it took until the following April for matters to be settled. Norah left just over £800, a modest but decent sum for the time, and four times the amount left by the supposedly prosperous parents of Alwyn Carr. It seems possible that the delay in settlement was caused by her uncertain status as a widow or otherwise, Benjamin having vanished. It does seem probable that if he had remained in touch with his family in England, there would be a record of his whereabouts and his death. But if anyone did know where he was, they kept it secret.

After Norah's death in 1929, Omar made a ring inscribed 'In Memory of Mother', which was lent anonymously to the 1973 exhibition of his work. The catalogue describes it as cast 18 carat gold, a dolphin entwined with a nymph who is clasping two pentagonal soft-edged emeralds. The catalogue states that the ring is one and three-eighths of an inch wide, surely another error, and that it was made for Omar's sister, though he only had brothers. Presumably the ring is still in private hands.

Wallace prospered in the United States; his American descendants say that his silverware was popular with movie stars, the only people in Hollywood or California with money to spare in the Depression years. The photograph shows an ornate tea set which he made for his daughter Mamie when she married Jack Lines in Los Angeles. It is still kept in the family, though it cannot be said to possess the simple elegant lines of his brother Omar's designs. Many descendants of Wallace and Beatrice now live in the USA though there are none with the Ramsden surname, Mamie having been the only grandchild.

In 1938 Wallace, Beatrice and Mamie returned to England for a visit. The family story of his prosperity is confirmed by the fact that they travelled on the *Queen Mary*, a great improvement in comfort on his first journey in steerage.[7] Four years earlier, when the large and luxurious

Above: Wallace Ramsden, Omar's brother, undated. (*Walt Ibbotson*)

Right: Tea service made by Wallace for his daughter Mamie's wedding to Jack Lines. (*Walt Ibbotson*)

Queen Mary had been launched, Omar had been commissioned to make the Staybrite (stainless steel) and silver-gilt casket presented to Her Majesty in honour of the occasion.

While in England they visited Lincolnshire where Beatrice and her siblings had been born and Omar went up to meet them. The postcard, taken by a beach photographer, shows them probably at Skegness or Mablethorpe, where they all got together. The picture of the group confirms the view that Omar enjoyed their company and was sociable and outgoing. He sent the postcard to a distant young cousin Sally in Canada. It shows, from left to right, Beatrice, Omar smoking as usual, Wallace, Mamie and Cissie (Clarissa) Ibbotson, Beatrice's sister. She had married Wallace's cousin Omar Ibbotson, son of Omar Pasha; their naming their own son Omar kept the name in the family. When Omar Ibbotson had retired from his ivory business in Sheffield in 1936, he and Cissie moved to Lincolnshire and set up a nursery garden which his grandson Robert Omar Ibbotson continues to run. At the end of the holiday, Wallace and family returned to the USA. It was to be their last meeting with Omar who died just a year later. Not one of the three brothers reached his three score years and ten. Mamie, the only descendant of the three, lived to the age of eighty-seven.

Omar kept the family connections with the USA throughout his life, his brothers were there, and his mother's closest sibling Elizabeth and her children, Omar's cousins, who travelled several times back and forth to England to keep in touch with family. Regarding his work, he was always keen to make the most of his association with the USA and exhibit there, he would have been proud to have it in museum and private collections. He continued to take an interest in the contemporary North American Arts and Crafts movements which flourished there until the end of his life.

Examples of his work were held in the Detroit Institute of Arts in Michigan, in the Cranbrook Academy of Arts near Detroit, in the Art Institute of Chicago and possibly other museums as well as in private collections, of which the best known latterly was probably the David

Beatrice, Omar smoking as usual, Wallace, Mamie, Cissie at the seaside, 1938.
(*Walt Ibbotson*)

and Vivian Campbell Collection.

The Detroit Society of Arts and Crafts was established in 1906, becoming a major venue of the influential American Arts and Crafts movement through exhibiting and selling; it was at its peak from about 1918 to 1929. Newspaper magnate George Gough Booth and other prominent citizens of the highly industrialised and wealthy city of Detroit took an active role in contributing to its foundation and success.[8] Booth and his wife had a great personal interest in Arts and Crafts and in 1908 had a house built for themselves at Cranbrook in the English Arts and Crafts style. In the following decades they added educational buildings and an Art Museum. It was on the outskirts of Detroit but was not intended to be in competition of any kind with the Detroit Institute.

The Cranbrook Archives include oddments of correspondence between Ramsden and Booth's representatives, which suggest that the former made several works which came to Detroit.[9] It seems that in 1921 George Booth bought a cigarette box by Ramsden and gifted it to the Institute, perhaps the one exhibited at the Liverpool Autumn Exhibition in that year. The box lid shows the Raleigh Ship and the side panels show scenes of Dawn and Sunset. The Institute returned the box to Booth at his request when he set up his own Cranbrook Art Museum. There was an overlap between activities of the Detroit Institute and the Cranbrook Educational Community and the wealthy George Booth appears to have played a central role in both.

Correspondence dated five years later, in Autumn 1926, between Ramsden and Miss Helen Plumb, discusses the possibility of commissioning a processional cross for Christ Church, Cranbrook to be gifted by Mr Booth. Miss Plumb was the Secretary to the Detroit Arts and Crafts Society and made several visits to England after World War I; it seems probable that she made the connection with Ramsden then and that George Booth had confidence in her taste and judgement. The order evidently went ahead and a personal letter from Ramsden to Miss Plumb on November 19 conveys how glad he is to have this opportunity of making the cross and asks her to tell Mr Booth that he will give of his best for him. Church records show a payment of $542.54 for the work which was delivered in the spring of 1927. However, in later church inventories the cross appears to be missing and its whereabouts remain a mystery.

Several other works by Ramsden were bought for the Cranbrook Museum in 1930, but unfortunately had to be sold in 1972 when the community was in financial difficulties. Records show the prices at which the pieces were bought in 1930 and sold on 2 May 1972 by Sotheby's in New York: a silver vase bought for $93 was sold for $500. The five other pieces, bought for a total of just over $120 were sold for $425, a 6 inch silver plate, two spoons, a beaker and a pen holder. The Cranbrook Museum Art Collection catalogue of 1930 also shows a silver goblet by Ramsden.[10]

In 1991 the Art Institute of Chicago acquired an early Ramsden and Carr bowl made in 1908. This particularly handsome work in silver contains a green glass bowl, attributed to James Powell and Sons, of

Whitefriars Glass Works, London. The possible function of the bowl has been much considered. In 1992 Ghenete Zelleke's monograph explored the Japanese stylistic influences on the design of the bowl, which has carp swimming through rippling water.[11]

Silver bowl, with glass interior by Powell, decorated with garnets and turquoises. Given by Richard T. Crane Junior in 1908. (*Courtesy of The Art Institute of Chicago*)

Many in Canada, as well as the USA, were very interested in Ramsden's work. His talk at Goldsmiths' Hall in 1928 had urged that to encourage the production of good, well-made silver, exhibitions on a large scale would be really advantageous. Nearly seventy years later, in 1997, Peter Kaellgren quoted this, describing how such exhibitions were held in Canada soon afterwards.[12]

Kaellgren's detailed article gives an interesting account of Ramsden's exhibits there, he identified over forty of those shown in the Canadian National Exhibition (CNE) by studying the workshop ledgers now held in the Goldsmiths' Company Archives. This was made easier where written descriptions supplemented sketches, costs, dates and names. It is not straightforward, however, as Ramsden often produced several very similar, though not identical, copies. Cigarette boxes decorated with a sailing ship, for example, were very popular in an age of heavy smoking.

Many variations of dishes and bowls of different sizes were made; beakers, goblets and flatware were always of interest and there must be many Canadian homes today with Ramsden pieces acquired through the CNE. Kaellgren pointed out that Ramsden might alter the name of a piece to appeal more to the Canadian market; for example what he called in his workbook a *Tiny Syrup Ladle* was renamed a *Maple Syrup Ladle*, and a cigarette casket originally named a Raleigh Ship was renamed *Jacques Cartier's Quest, A.D. 1535*. When Scottish paintings were a particular feature of the 1931 exhibition, Ramsden displayed several condiment sets and small items of flatware decorated with the Scottish thistle. A pretty teaspoon of this kind is part of the Museums Sheffield collection.

The Canadian National Exhibition was the largest annual fair in the world at that time. Kaellgren records that Ramsden displayed no fewer than 141 pieces, from small gold cufflinks in 1923 to a large vase and cover surmounted by St George in 1926; they were among the most expensive items displayed. His highest and lowest priced pieces were shown in 1931, a fruit dish costing $380 and a butter spreader costing $4.75. In all he showed work in the CNE nine times between 1922 and 1934. As well as opportunities for sales, his reputation for handmade, good quality English silverware would have been enhanced. Ramsden had private commissions from wealthy Canadians too, for example the silver *Fauns and Dryads Bowl*, for Waldo W. Skinner of Montreal.

In April 1939, shortly before he died, his work was exhibited at the prestigious New York World's Fair, the biggest international event since

World War I, visited by 44 million people. Again, the Sheffield press was amongst the many who recorded this; The Star, in its Northern Folk in London section wrote that Ramsden 'was represented by a cup and bowl lent for the occasion by Mr Montague Norman'. Ramsden was quite unwell by this time, but continued working right up to the week of his death in August, his reputation was now truly global.

1 British Army WWI Service Records, 1914–1920.

2 New York Passenger Lists, 1820–1957, *Berengaria*, 1923.

3 US Federal Census, Los Angeles, 1930.

4 ibid, 1940.

5 May 1928, Horace and Dolly Ramsden, *Laurentia*, Montreal to the UK. September 1928, returned on *Minnekhada* to New York.

6 *Laconia*, Cunard Line 25 May 1929, Liverpool to New York.

7 SS *Queen Mary*, Passenger Lists, 1938.

8 Letter from James W. Tottis, Acting Curator of American Art, Detroit Institute of Arts, to Paul Hallam, 14 February 2000. PHA.

9 Correspondence and notes from Amy James, Archivist, Cranbrook Archives, Michigan, 7 March 2000. PHA.

10 Catalogue of Cranbrook Museum Art Collection, 1930, p27, no. 312 Copy PHA.

11 Ghenete Zelleke, 1992.

12 *Omar Ramsden and the CNE, Material Culture Review,* 1997, then in *The Silver Society of Canada Journal*, Fall 1998 No 1, Vol 1. Peter Kaellgren of the Royal Ontario Museum.

CHAPTER 12

The End of an Era: Ramsden's Death and a Family Falling-out

In 1928 Omar had written one of his few known personal letters, he was enjoying married life. He and Anne had just returned from 'a most wonderful holiday: perhaps the most beautiful one I have ever had. Sweden is lovely!' This letter was to an unnamed Ibbotson cousin, of whom he had at least twenty, who was interested in an Ibbotson crest. Ramsden said that he had made a lifelong study of heraldry but did not know the crest spoken of. He wrote:

> In fact my maternal mother's forebears[the Ibbotsons] seem to have been Dungworth farmers for ages until your Gt. Grandfather and my G.F. left home and started ivorycutting in Sheffield.

He concluded that they are 'hardly likely to be armigeous'. [sic] Dungworth was a few miles outside Sheffield.[1]

Life was going well; marriage was suiting Ramsden and his reputation was at its peak, with commissions and sales coming in from all over the globe. His achievements were recognised by his being awarded the 'Freedom of the City of London' in the Company of Goldsmiths' in February 1929. The Sheffield press continued to follow the activities of their famous son with interest throughout the 1930s. Another of Paul Hallam's cuttings from 1931 show a journalist had obviously visited St Dunstan's previously:

LONDON EXHIBITION, ARTIST CRAFTSMAN
Sheffield Man's Great Work

Some Sheffield people might not know it, but the city has produced a great artist craftsman in Mr Omar Ramsden. Born in Sheffield he was apprenticed for seven years to a firm of Sheffield goldsmiths. 'At the end of that time,' he told me when I interviewed him in his tastefully appointed house in Kensington today, '...I got out of Sheffield as soon as I possibly could, because I realised there was no opening for a craftsman there because Sheffield is a city of manufacturers. It is thirty four years since I left Sheffield, where I studied the art of the goldsmith and silversmith'.

For having taught him so much, Mr Ramsden is grateful to his native city, though, as an artist, he has little use for mass-production work.

In his oak-panelled dining room today, with an old fashioned log fire emitting a sweet scent into the room, art treasures of his own original design and craftsmanship, worth, in the aggregate, many thousands of pounds, shone brightly as they reflected the light from shaded electric lamps; things of beauty and vertu which caused people he had invited to view them to exclaim aloud in admiration.

Speaking of present-day craftsmanship, he said it was passing through a crisis. 'There is no doubt,' he added, 'that people who make things by mass production are taking much more care over their work than they used to, and to be made by hand is not necessarily a virtue unless a thing is supremely well made.

There can never be any point of contact between mass production and the work of the artist. There are people who say they should work together, but they are just like oil and vinegar, excellent ingredients in their way, but they do not mix. The craftsman works for the connoisseur, the manufacturer for the million. The artist has the joy of creating, the manufacturer has only the joy of making money. The manufacturer should not be jealous of the craftsman.'

Whilst Omar's reputation continued to grow, so did his adoptive family: his step-daughter Joan who had lived in St Dunstan's since she was a small child, became engaged to Dr James Henry Lascelles Gilmore of Acre Lane, SW2, in May 1932. She was 25 and named as the daughter of Mrs Omar Ramsden and the late Charles Downs Butcher. Forbidden by her mother to join the theatre, she had become a nurse and met James Gilmore through her work. Dr Gilmore bought a practice in Abingdon and a house in Park Crescent, where a son was born to him and Joan in 1933 and a daughter two years later.

1933 brought another family wedding. Either through his work, or through Cumberbatch commissions to Omar, Omar's stepson Gerald met the writer's cousin Pamela, who was on the stage, and mixing in smart theatrical circles. She was a great friend of Cecil Beaton's daughter and their 'set' was considered very 'advanced'; she and her sister Sylvia, who danced at Covent Garden, went about together in a motorcycle and side car, which was very modern for the time and would no doubt have met with the approval of their forward-looking aunt Alice, the aviator. The photograph by society photographer Dorothy Wilding was taken during the period of her marriage to Gerald.

Pamela and Sylvia lived with their parents Lily and George Simpson-Willins in Woodfield House in Ealing. Lily, although the older sibling, was under the thumb of her dictatorial sister Alice, with her strong opinions on all matters, family and otherwise. However, Alice did approve of the match between her niece and Gerald and an announcement was made in *The Times* on 10 June 1933:

> The marriage arranged between Gerald Downs Butcher and Pamela Willins will take place on June 17th at St Mary's, The Boltons, [near Seymour Place] at 12 noon. All friends will be welcome at the church.

St Mary's was one of many churches with an altar cross and candlesticks designed and made by Ramsden. Presumably the Cumberbatch family, the Willins, Ramsden and the Downs Butchers all came together to celebrate and enjoy the family wedding. However, the outcome of the marriage was not happy, it was to be the first of Gerald's three

Photograph by Dorothy Wilding of Gerald's first wife Pamela, undated. (*Eliza Buckingham, Pamela's daughter*)

unsuccessful marriages, annulled three years later on the grounds of non-consummation. The resulting publicity caused Pamela to retreat from London to rural Norfolk for a time, and she bore the name of Mrs Downs-Butcher unwillingly until her re-marriage in January 1939. She made a lasting marriage, though her daughter Eliza relates that Gerald's name was not allowed to be mentioned in their household. Gerald moved back to St Dunstan's.

Gerald Downs Butcher, actor/manager, undated. (*Simon Gilmore*)

His oldest nephew Christopher Gilmore remembers Gerald as always grumbling and very irritable, but musical and good at crosswords and cricket. Christopher remembers the promise of a shilling from him if he could sing 'The Swan' from beginning to end, and the thrill of being taken backstage in the theatre, which encouraged him towards a career of his own in drama. His niece Anne remembers finding him rather attractive and debonair.

Throughout 1938 and 1939 Ramsden's health had been failing. Like many at the time he was a heavy smoker, in almost all the family photos he is holding a cigarette or pipe. As his health declined, his workbooks became noticeably less detailed and precise than before, reflecting his diminishing attention to detail. But nevertheless it was unexpected when he died, aged sixty-five, at home in his bed at St Dunstan's, on Wednesday 9 August 1939. He had been working as usual in the preceding week. He was found by his stepson Gerald who registered his death the following day. The cause was recorded as 'a) Coronary occlusion, b) arterio sclerosis'. His funeral was arranged by J. H. Kenyon and Co., (coincidentally more cousins of the writer) and his remains were cremated in Golders Green Crematorium only two days later, on Friday 11 August.[2] His ashes were dispersed in the garden of the crematorium, though there is no memorial.

These bare facts took a long time to find. The *Dictionary of National Biography* is incorrect, stating that Ramsden was buried in Eccleshall, Sheffield. I travelled the couple of hundred miles to Sheffield and spent a whole day in the archives, searching for a record of his burial, looking in an ever-expanding circle at church and cemetery burial records, but there was no sign of him. Returning home, I then researched all the burials in churches and cemeteries near his home, to no avail. Later, talking to Paul Hallam, he said he thought he had a recollection of a cremation in Golders Green Crematorium in North London, quite some miles from St Dunstan's. I got in touch with them and at last! The record of his cremation there shows Friday, 11 August 1939.

A short announcement of his death was made in *The Times* Personal Column on Monday, 14 August, noting only his name, date and home address, plus simply 'RIP.' The announcement was not made until after his cremation, apparently in accordance with his wishes. Like his marriage, things seem to have been done with a business-like formality and little room for sentiment.

There were several lengthy obituaries in the national and Sheffield press in the following weeks, and in *The Jeweller and Metalworker* and the

Goldsmiths' Journal. The *Daily Telegraph* and *Morning Post* of 15 August began:

> Few men in recent years can have perpetuated the art of the goldsmith more effectively than Mr Omar Ramsden, whose death has occurred in London at the age of sixty-five.

In the eight inches of column dedicated to him, several of his best-known works are mentioned, including this:

> To celebrate the completion of the Irak [sic] pipe-line in 1935 he executed, after a visit there, a casket of oriental design, consisting of 90oz of silver and 10oz of gold for presentation to King Ghazi.'

Like other journalists this writer attributes desires to him, perhaps not always with complete accuracy: '...he had as a young man one great ambition – to carry on the mediaeval art of the ceremonial goldsmith'. The *Sheffield Telegraph* and *Independent* of 15 August, referred to him as 'the world's greatest craftsman of his time, who was indeed called the modern Cellini.' Had this writer read Ramsden's views on Cellini he might have chosen another analogy. It continued:

> He died in his sleep the same day he had been hard at work. In a charming little house which he designed for himself on 13th century lines in a backwater of south-west London, Omar Ramsden performed the most exquisite work in gold and silver that modern eyes have seen.

Of particular interest in this obituary is that on this date, 15 August 1939, the journalist was still able to write with accuracy: 'It was Omar Ramsden who made the Peace Bowl which was presented by an anonymous Englishman to Mr Neville Chamberlain after he saved the world from war last September.'

This was a reference to the speech following the Munich Agreement wherein Chamberlain declared 'Peace for our time'. But just five weeks after this article was written, Britain declared war on Germany, one might say the Peace Bowl was made in vain, or at least in unfulfilled hope. The obituary went on to describe the dramatic effects which Ramsden was reputed to enjoy:

His own home was like something out of the Arabian Nights. The walls of the house – which stands on the site of Nell Gwynne's fig garden – have hidden cupboards lined with treasures of exquisite beauty... Swinging back a panel which looked solid, Ramsden would show you shelves filled with silver dishes and golden goblets beautifully fashioned. He had a kit of over a thousand chisels, some of them very tiny. He was a staunch opponent of machinery.

The last phrase is not entirely true, he used machinery judiciously, and his lecture to the Goldsmiths' Company in March 1928 explained his thoughts on the matter. This is just one example of ideas being attributed to him which he never expressed:

Let our artist-craftsmen and our designers be given liberty to study and to think out new and splendid ideas both for handwork and machinery.

The obituaries in *The Times* on 15 and 17 August are sweeping in a similar way, '…He devoted himself entirely to the revival of the art of the English ceremonial goldsmith'. It went on to describe several of his most well-known works:

When Major Astor, MP and Lady Violet Astor were presented with the Freedom of Dover in 1933 the oak and silver caskets in which the scrolls were contained were the work of Omar Ramsden. The wood was reputed to have been taken from Nelson's Victory during some repairs made about thirty five years earlier.

The famous *Three Kings Mazer Bowl* was mentioned, with its representations of George V, Edward VIII, and George VI. 'In 1937 he made a mazer bowl to mark the fact that Britain had three kings in a twelve month. It was described as one of the world's outstanding works in gold'.

Sheffield's newspaper, *The Star*, wrote: [3]

STAR MAN'S DIARY, Bouverie Street, Monday:

After his death, notice of his passing was kept till after cremation, in accordance with his wishes...Ramsden would receive a bank clerk's small commission with the respect that he would pay to the King's command.

It meant a visit to his house, a quiet straightforward question: 'Exactly how much do you want to pay?' and a discussion of the design and amount of workmanship within that figure. Business over, he would offer one a glass of sherry and a cigarette and discuss, sometimes for an hour or more, the world at large, and, above all, his favourite recreation, the drama.

In due course the drawing would arrive; and then the finished article, of a beauty that made its recipient wonder whatever the price had had to do with it ...The price, indeed, was beside the point. Ramsden might have smashed the edges of a score of chisels in etching a rose on a white-gold engagement ring, and the cost in craftsmanship might have been for millionaires only....

...his craft and spirit were finely made in a goblet he once made out of six ounces of gold brought to him by Lord Lee of Fareham. When his lordship received the goblet he found chiselled around a green stone at the bottom of it the words:

WISDOM CANNOT BE GOTTEN FOR GOLD

After his death an exhibition of some of his work was held in the Sheffield Weston Park Museum:

ART IN SILVER

Mr J. W. Baggaley, Director of the Museum, who was well acquainted with Mr Ramsden, told *The Star* today of three valuable pieces which have been acquired by the museum at different times. They are all of silver, and include a chalice, richly worked, a loving cup ... and a flower vase and cover. Mr Ramsden named many of his pieces, and the latter he termed 'Cupid's Throne'.

Mr Baggaley said Mr Ramsden was a frequent visitor to the Weston Park Museum and often lectured there.

Only weeks after Omar's death, World War II began. Anne never reconciled herself to her loss, she had enjoyed being Omar's wife, at the centre of interest and creative activity and travelling abroad with him. She had made a dramatic figure as she went about Kensington dressed in her cape with her silver headed cane, assuming an aura of grandeur, and often wearing the Pilgrim's Girdle. Omar too was an elegant dresser when away from the workshop, as can be seen from the photographs; he also sported a cape on social occasions.

Anne Ramsden, nee Berriff, formerly Downs Butcher, undated. (*Simon Gilmore*)

By September 1940 she was living in Abingdon with her daughter Joan and Joan's two children, Christopher and Anne. About this time she gave Leslie Durbin various patterns which Omar had used in the workshop, on condition that he never sold them. He kept faithfully to his promise and they were passed on to the Goldsmiths' Company Archive.

Joan's husband Dr Gilmore joined the armed forces and spent most of the war in Burma. Partly because of the war and partly for young Christopher's health, Joan, her two children and Anne moved temporarily from Abingdon to a cottage, *Teathes*, in Kirkland near Whitehaven in Cumbria. Sharing the household was not a success. Christopher was sent unwillingly away to school and the three females lived together in the cottage. Christopher remembers Anne and her daughter being great rivals, and rowing continually. Anne spent a great deal of her time digging in the garden and growing vegetables, not something she had ever done before. The impression of Anne Ramsden given by her grandchildren is of a domineering and autocratic woman who was distant and haughty, always with more time for the males of the family than the females.

She doted on her son Gerald and the feeling was mutual, but family accounts suggest that neither her daughter nor granddaughter appeared of much interest to her and received little of her attention. Her grandson Christopher was rather dazzled and in awe of her, she was well-travelled, well dressed, cultured, with a great interest in literature and drama, particularly Shakespeare. He admired her from a distance; she was never a fond or affectionate grandmother, but intimidating to both children.

Early in the war, in 1940, Gerald changed his name by Deed Poll, his father Charles Downs Butcher had been dead for thirteen years.[4] It appears that Gerald had always disliked his surname, having been teased at school by being called 'Butcher-Baker-Candlestick Maker'. Gerald took his mother's maiden name of Berriff, adding an 'e' at the end.

He had just married then for a second time, four years after the end of his first marriage. He married twenty year-old Alkie Craig, seventeen years his junior, but this second marriage was no more successful than the first. After some years Alkie gave birth to twins, but in registering their births, very unusually in the official Register of Births, Deaths and Marriages, the entry of their names was made twice. The first entry for each of them was 'Berriffe', her husband's surname. Immediately below this they are entered once again with the same Christian names but with the surname 'Fournier'. This very unusual practice could suggest that their father's name was Fournier even though she was married to Berriffe, and that later the twins would be able to choose which name to use. In fact, it appears they did go on to use the name of Fournier.

After the war years in Cumberland Joan and the children returned to Park Crescent, Abingdon, their father returned from active service and he and Joan had two more sons. Omar's widow moved in with the family, but the arrangement was no happier than the previous one in Cumbria. The children were always to remember the tense atmosphere in the house, the constant arguments and the raised voices of Joan and her mother. Anne had her own rooms on the top floor with the beautiful furniture which had come from Ramsden. She kept her room locked, only joining the family for meals. Christopher recollects her eating her meals sitting on the stairs after there had been a row. Perhaps she was bitter and resentful about the way her life had diminished when Omar died. After some time, she moved out of the house to the Abingdon Road in Oxford and refused to have anything to do with her daughter or grandchildren. She returned to a house of her own in Abingdon only in her final years.

Gerald married yet again, this time to Vanda Rinaldi, in the spring of 1946. After five years she gave birth to a son who bore the Berriffe name. That marriage did not last either and in time Vanda married someone else. This marital history could suggest that he was homosexual, but as homosexual activity was illegal perhaps Gerald felt that marriage was the only acceptable option available to him. In due course, he moved to Italy where he became a Director of Studies at the British Institute in Rome, and died at the age of 82.

Anne Ramsden died in Abingdon in 1950, her ashes were scattered in Oxford Crematorium according to her wish. Her death was reported in *The Times* Personal column: 'On April 16 1950 after a short illness, in her 77th year, Annie Emily, widow of Omar Ramsden (artist goldsmith), late of St Dunstan's, Seymour Walk, SW10'. She had survived Omar by eleven years, and her first husband by 23 years.

Her will was brief, she left everything, amounting to £27,490, to Gerald, a considerable sum at a time when the house in Park Crescent would have cost about £2000.[5] It had all come from Omar, her first husband's estate having amounted to 'nil'. The only note of interest in the will was that Gerald should 'use continually my dower chest, as a tribute to its maker', probably Ramsden.

Her son-in-law James, a General Practitioner in the town, was present at her death, so had evidently kept in touch with her despite being divorced from her daughter; he was the informant on her death certificate. The anger and tension in the Abingdon household cannot have helped the relationship between Joan and James. There was great upset in the family when James had an affair with a patient, which attracted a lot of publicity from the *News of the World*. Joan and James parted, he married his patient and had more children.

Joan's name was not even mentioned in her mother's will, reflecting the bitter feelings between them. One wonders what Omar might have thought of this exclusion of Joan, he had always been fond of her and all the family photos show them on relaxed and comfortable terms. Had Anne pre-deceased Omar, both his stepchildren would have benefited directly and substantially. Joan would have received 'all my interest in Grove Cottage, Seymour Place', the house adjoining St Dunstan's Studio which he must have acquired. Gerald was to receive the residue of Omar's estate, after gifts of £1,000 to Jeanne Étève, £200 to Albert Ulyett, his long-term manager and £100 to Walter Andrews, his foreman.

Had his wife and stepson died before him his workmen would have had their bequests and Joan and Jeanne would have shared the rest of his estate equally. But as Omar died before Annie, none of these bequests had to be made, and Annie inherited the whole estate, about £13,000. According to her offspring, she lived the rest of her life embittered and unhappy.

1 Family letter from Omar to an un-named cousin, unpublished.

2 Golders Green Crematorium, Cremation No. 46319, Cremation Date, 11.08.1939.

3 *The Star*, 14 August, 1939

4 *London Gazette*, 30 April 1940

5 Anne Ramsden Will, 1940

CHAPTER 13

Alwyn Carr's Death and Will

Alwyn Carr was to survive Omar by one year. He made his detailed nine-page will in January 1938, when he was sixty-six. He appointed as executors an army officer with whom he had served in the RASC in the Great War, his brother Arthur and niece Joan Carr. More than any other known document, it gave me a picture of Carr, his life and loyalties.[1]

He left very specific instruction for a Roman Catholic burial in Little Marlow Cemetery and for the design of his grave. Of personal bequests, all the ecclesiastical vessels he owned were left to poor Catholic or Anglican churches at the discretion of his trustees or the Church Crafts League. Lieutenant Colonel Rowe was left 'my silver and jade flower vase and my St Dunstan's wine cup'.

To his niece Joan he left domestic objects which she had perhaps admired, his silver tea service and Spode china from Melbury Road and his corner cupboard and seven mahogany chairs from Bourne End. Her brother Alwyn Paul was to receive his gold cufflinks, gold and silver cigarette cases, gold watches, grandfather clock, a big chair with a pineapple on the back and a Savonarola Florentine chair with initials. Some of these pieces can be seen in the 1914 photographs of St Dunstan's Studio. Alwyn Paul also inherited the portrait of his great grandfather Joseph Ellison, mentioned previously, and Alwyn's War Service Medals.

The Victoria & Albert Museum was to choose any works 'in silver or other metals and such of my drawings and photographs' that they wanted from all those in Melbury Road, to be selected by the museum director within a year of his death. Alwyn listed those pieces he thought most suitable, together with precise instructions about who was to be offered them should the museum decline them. He also specified that they were to be 'for permanent exhibition', a clause that was later to prove problematic.

He suggested they choose the case of twelve silver spoons of early English Saints, a silver cream jug set with turquoise, the electrotypes of the Armada Bowl and the cup given by London University to Paris University, silver wine cups and a claret jug, and the original designs for the London University Mace and the Westminster Cathedral Monstrance and bronze model. The choice of these items would strongly suggest that he personally had played the major role in their design.

Looking at the present Victoria & Albert Museum collection, I found that it held none of these gifts. In order to understand why this was so, Eric Turner, present Curator of Metalwork Collections at the museum examined the correspondence between Mr Bailey, Keeper of Metalwork at the time, and Carr's solicitors on behalf of the executors. It reveals that Bailey had declined to accept the gifts, at first because of the difficulty of providing permanent exhibition space. In due course, the executors agreed to waive this condition, but by then Bailey had decided to accept only one piece, a plain silver beaker of 1914–5, 'notwithstanding that this is a joint work of Captain Carr and Mr Omar Ramsden'.

Eric Turner suggests that it may be possible that the reason Bailey was unwilling to accept the bequest was that Museum policy at the time discouraged the acceptance of contemporary silver. Further, Bailey did not have any personal interest in that area of collecting. Perhaps acceptance of the simple beaker was merely a gesture of goodwill on his part. He and Carr were very likely to have been acquainted as both were members of the Goldsmiths' Company. Thus it is that, very unfortunately, the Museum missed the opportunity to own several of Carr's pieces, in addition to his drawings and photographs, and they remained in his family, their present whereabouts unknown for the most part, though the early English saints spoons were recently sold by John Bull Antiques and J. B. Silverware.

Alwyn's grave in Little Marlow cemetery, 2016. (*Nick Chapman*)

Arthur Hughes, Carr's partner of many years, was at first left domestic effects at Bourne End to the value of £50 and any of Alwyn's wearing apparel he would like; any clothes unwanted by Arthur were to go to the Crusade of Rescue and Homes for Destitute Catholic Children. Arthur was also to receive the sum of £250, and an annuity of £78. The whole bequest to Arthur was substantially increased in a codicil which Alwyn added to his will a few days before his death two years later. All the remaining furniture and household effects were to be shared by his niece, nephew, and brother Arthur.

Other bequests show his attachment to the Roman Catholic Church; he left £200 to his local church in High Street, Kensington – Our Lady of Victories – for masses to be said over the following ten years for the repose of his soul, with a further £50 for their general use. The church was to have great need of money; only a few weeks after Carr's death it was destroyed by four incendiary bombs and not long afterwards three more German bombs landed within a hundred yards of his Melbury Road studio.[2]

A further £50 was left to the Catholic Church nearest to Bourne End at the time, in Marlow, and £100 to the Crusade of Rescue. But his major gift was a legacy of £5,000 to the Diocese of Northampton, for the building of a Catholic church in Bourne End. He expressed a hope that it would be dedicated to St Dunstan, and it was. The years of World War II intervened and it was sixteen years before the church was built. During those years, the costs had changed substantially so that when construction finally began in 1955, it had to be a very simple design, literally built by the hands of the parishioners to keep within budget.[3] That building is now used as the church hall, as a permanent St Dunstan's was built adjoining it in 1979.

The Artists Rifles Memorial Fund, the Art Workers Guild and the May Queen Cross and Chain Memorial Fund at Whitelands College, Putney were left £100 each.

The residue of his estate was essentially left to his brother Arthur, and the children of his brother William, namely Joan and Alwyn Paul Carr. He noted that he left nothing to William and his wife as '…I appreciate what devoted parents they have been and I think it will give them more pleasure that I have endeavoured to do something for their children'. Like his uncle, Alwyn Paul joined the army when World War II broke out, becoming a Lieutenant and being awarded the Military Cross in 1944.[4] Unfortunately Alwyn was not alive then to see his nephew receive the honour.

His final personal note in his will was 'To Omar Ramsden… my friend and partner for so many years my continuous affection and gratitude for all that I owe to him during our years together'. In Alwyn's more fulfilling new life with Arthur Hughes, he had long left behind any resentful or bitter feelings. As Omar died a year before Carr, eighteen months after the will was written, he probably never received this final affectionate message.

While in hospital, just six days before his death, Alwyn added a codicil to his will, witnessed by two of the hospital nurses. Once again, he gave his own address as St Dunstan's, Melbury Road and Arthur

Hughes' as St Dunstan's, Bourne End, never publicly the same for both of them. One of the main changes he made was to substantially increase his bequests to Hughes and to appoint him a joint executor and trustee of his estate with his brother and niece. Whereas Hughes had previously been left furniture to the value of £50 and any of Carr's wearing apparel he could use, this was increased to all his books and half of the furniture and domestic effects at St Dunstan's, Bourne End. He increased his gift to Hughes from £250 to £500, and declared that the loan he had made to Hughes in 1936 for the Dilloway Printing Company was now to be considered a gift not be repaid. His final generous bequest to Hughes was to increase the annuity he had left him from £78 yearly to £100. These bequests surely demonstrate the long-standing affection between the two.

Having lived about five years at St Dunstan's, Abbotsbrook, Alwyn Carr died on 22 April 1940, in the King Edward VII Hospital in Windsor, one year after Omar Ramsden; he was just sixty-eight years old. Probate was granted in June that year to his brother, 'Arthur Carr, private tutor, Arthur Henry Hughes, Master Printer and Joan Carr, spinster'. He left £20,413 16s 4d. At the time of his death he and Arthur Hughes were dividing their time between 2b Melbury Road, where both had been registered as electors for the last fourteen years, and Alwyn's house in Bourne End.

Alwyn was buried on 26 April according to his wishes in the Little Marlow Cemetery in Bourne End.[5] The Clerk to the Parish Council searched through the Burial Registers to find his plot, and we eventually found his grave in a quiet corner. It was just as his precise instructions had requested. Over his grave he had wanted:

> Erected as a memorial in hard and enduring stone (not marble) of a simple and dignified compact design introducing the Cross and Sword and my device 'a winged hammer in a shield' such memorial not to be too big the same to be designed by Mr Laurence Turner or some other member of the Art Workers Guild.

He allowed a good sum of money for this, obviously aesthetic interests were important to him in death as they were in life. Beautifully carved around the sides of the memorial are the fitting words from Psalm 26:8:

I have loved, O Lord, the beauty of thy house, and the place where thy glory dwelleth.

His device of a winged hammer is at the foot, and the cross and sword on the top surface.

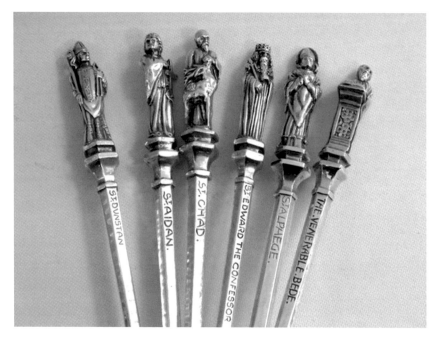

Dessert spoons decorated with saints of the early English church,
mentioned in Carr's will 1912–1914.
(*Photo courtesy of John Bull Antiques and J. B. Silverware*)

In December of the year Alwyn died Arthur Hughes was still living at St Dunstan's, Bourne End, and gave this address when he bought the plot adjoining Alwyn's grave. But it seems probable that he bought it to allow a generous space around it rather than to be interred in it himself, especially as Alwyn's brother Arthur bought the plot on the other side a couple of years later. In his own will forty years later Arthur Hughes expressed a wish to be buried near his parents in the village of Rowde, Wiltshire, where he was born. The search for Hughes' grave caused a great deal of confusion to Gloria, the Parish Clerk, and myself. Unaware then that Arthur Hughes had lived on for so many years, when we came across 'Arthur Hughes' buried just a few yards from Alwyn we assumed it was 'our' Hughes. It took the intervention of the 'real' Arthur *Henry* Hughes's great nephew Tom Hughes to put me back on the right track, and to remind me of what I really knew, to double check every fact however obvious it might seem, before assuming its truth.

Arthur Henry Hughes stayed on at St Dunstan's for quite some time, and Alwyn's brother Arthur Carr moved in with his wife Dora, the three of them living harmoniously together. Hughes' niece Betty remembered that Hughes later moved out into the converted stables of a house in Bourne End, where she and her cousin would visit him as children. In 1946–7 he is thought to have lived at The Bower House in the village. Arthur Carr lived on at St Dunstan's until his death there in 1949. He had appointed Hughes, who now had a new partner, as an executor of his own will, so presumably they continued to get along well. Arthur's widow Dora (or Doretta as Betty remembered her) lived on there at least until 1957 when her name is on a schedule of properties. It seems she became increasingly blind; a lady companion lived there with her while the house deteriorated around them. The house was sold in about 1960 and Dora died in 1962 in Maidenhead.

By the strangest coincidence a novel, or 'free fantasia on a friend's life', namely *Pilcrow* by Adam Mars-Jones, has a central character whose family moved into the house when he was a child, it was they who changed its name from St Dunstan's. It was bought by his father from 'two half blind old ladies'. The novel begins with the sentence, 'The spring I learned to drive, the cherry tree in front of our house in Bourne End flowered as never before. It was 1968'.[6] The cherry tree is still there and the outlook from the front of the house looking towards the small stream and bridge is still recognisable as the one Arthur Hughes painted.

1 Alwyn Carr's Will, January 1938, Codicil added April 1940.
2 www.bombsite.org, viewed 8 December 2015.
3 The *Evening News*, Spring 1956 (no date), *The Maidenhead Advertiser*, 13 and 20 April, 1956
4 Military Service Records 134616
5 Parish Burial Records, Little Marlow, 1940
6 *Pilcrow* Adam Mars-Jones, p223, Faber and Faber, 2008

CHAPTER 14

Setting the Record Straight

Even after the many obituaries of 1939, several mentions of Ramsden's name, though very few of Carr's, occur in the press, particularly *The Times* of London, over the years up to the present.

In 1941, after Carr's death, Sheffield Museum held an exhibition of his and Ramsden's work. Carr had expressed a wish that the City Museum in Sheffield, then at Weston Park, now part of Museums Sheffield, should receive 'a selection of pieces from his treasure chest'. Accordingly, the curator of the museum, Mr Baggaley, visited London and had the responsibility of selecting eight examples, seven with the partners' joint mark and one with Carr's own mark. As usual it is very difficult to decide on the individual contribution of each partner, in design and/or making, of any of the pieces from the partnership period. It seems reasonable to expect that the pieces Carr possessed at the time of his death were those he had had a major part in designing, in spite of the joint mark. The previous year, Omar's widow Anne had presented the museum with the copper model of the jewel and collar for the Honourable Company of Master Mariners.

The *Goldsmiths' Journal* described the works presented by the legatees: those with the joint marks of the partnership were the silver bowl of 1899, with the Spenser quotation, two works 'in the Persian style' – a bowl of 1917 and a box with a lid of 1916. A 1917 goblet, a silver bowl of the same year with a band of oak leaves, plus a small caddy spoon and a sugar sifter, completed the items. Alwyn's own work was a bowl, with a lid ornamented with green stones.[1]

These pieces, with Ramsden's loving cup named *The Rose Bower*, his book of sketches and some beautiful small spoons from the Bill Brown Collection, comprise the majority of the pieces in Museums Sheffield today. Additionally, in Sheffield are the city mace in the Town Hall; the wax model for the key in Hallam University and the two silver chalices and patens bequeathed to St Cecilia's and now in the church of St Bernard of Clairvaux.

In December 1943 it was probably Omar's widow who advertised the family silver for sale.[2] Following Omar's death, and her much more restricted life, Anne probably no longer felt a need for it.

Four years later, as already mentioned, in a notice in *The Times*, Ramsden's widow published a statement giving Leslie Durbin permission to 'Carry on the tradition' of her late husband's work, to help him establish his new business with Leonard Moss. As he said himself, '... once the workshop is installed, there is the problem of living until a demand has been established for the production of that workshop'.[3]

Anne's help must have been welcome, as a couple of years later, in 1949, under 'Exhibitions' in *The Times* was a notice 'Hand-wrought silver by Leslie Durbin at St Dunstan's ... (former home of Omar Ramsden)'.[4]

Reviews of Ramsden's work have continued to be written over the decades, though Carr's name is seldom mentioned nor his input into the partnership period acknowledged. In July 1951, *The Times* Museums Correspondent reviewed an Exhibition of Modern British Silverwork, held at Goldsmiths' Hall. He wrote that within Ramsden's period he was the 'chief personality... whose work is fully represented by, among other things, two pieces commissioned from him by Queen Mary – a cup in 1916 [note that this is still the partnership period] and a bowl in 1933 – and by a cup given in 1923 to the Oxford and Cambridge Golfing Society by the President of the United States Golfing Association'.[5]

A letter to the editor in July 1954 from F.W. Tomlinson of Sandwich, Kent, participated in what seems to be an ongoing correspondence on the subject of enamelling. He pointed out that:

Mr Omar Ramsden, about thirty years ago, made several silver and enamel plaques to be placed under The Buffs' old colours in the Warriors' Chapel in Canterbury Cathedral, describing in what campaigns they had been carried by Battalions of The Buffs ... More recently a similar one was made by Mr Leslie Durbin.

In the 1960s jewellery by Ramsden could be bought for relatively modest prices. A saleroom correspondent of *The Times* in October 1966 reported the sale of a silver pendant of St Beatrix for £50, by 'the well-known Edwardian jeweller Omar Ramsden'.

Over the years, many mentions of him occur in connection with sales. His name on a piece has generally added quite a lot to the financial value of an otherwise fairly ordinary domestic article. Good quality pieces have always been seen to be a good investment. In the 'Personal Investment and Finance' section of *The Times* in July 1973 Charles du Cann wrote a balanced article on the 'Shining reputation of Ramsden silver', from the point of view of an investor or collector. He wrote that 'There is no biography of Ramsden', but he hoped the present article would 'enable the private investor or aspiring collector to judge the enduring value of this silversmith's work...' He commented that it was not easy to acquire pieces at the time of writing as 'specimens are tightly held by enthusiastic and industrious collectors'.

> Our greatest English silversmiths, like Paul de Lamerie and Paul Storr, never attained anything approaching the mystique that Omar Ramsden enjoyed during his lifetime, and still holds. It is admitted, even by his critics who give more credit to his employees than to the maître himself, that he revolutionised English silver craftsmanship and production.

This is a direct reference to the critique of the same year in the Birmingham Catalogue.

In 1975, described as a 'curiosity' in a Sotheby sale room report in *The Times*, was the sale of a silver and parcel-gilt girdle the writer thought was almost certainly made for Ramsden's wife, though being hallmarked 1925 it pre-dates her marriage to Ramsden. She certainly possessed the linked chain girdle decorated with scenes from the Pilgrim's Way to Canterbury. It was sold at £420, and in 1978 was gifted to the British Museum by Professor and Mrs Hull Grundy, with five other Ramsden and Carr pieces.

Unexpectedly, an entry for 'Omar Ramsden' appeared in the sports category of *The Times* in October 1982. This was the name given to an American bred horse from Guy Harwood's Pulborough stable, who had 'shone' in the Ruswarp Maiden Stakes at Redcar on the previous day. Presumably Ramsden had an enthusiastic admirer in the horse-racing world.

In the summer of 1984, the Spink auction house held a London exhibition of *60 Years of English Silver*, from 1878 to 1938, in which some work by Ramsden was included.[6] An interesting personal recollection of him in the mid-1930s by Mrs Alison Pierson was included in the accompanying booklet:

> We went to see him with a view to buying a first wedding anniversary present for each other but were persuaded to order twelve goblets, the design of each one representing an event in our lives. Each goblet weighed nearly 6 oz. and cost four and a half guineas. To spread the cost we asked Ramsden to let us have two at a time to celebrate various anniversaries, with my mother helping out at Christmas and birthdays. Living in Baghdad, we took our ideas to him whenever we came on leave and then before returning to Iraq we collected the finished articles. The final display of these twelve goblets on our dinner table had no equal.
>
> Omar Ramsden had a half-basement workshop/studio called St Dunstan's (after the patron saint of goldsmiths) in Seymour Walk off the Fulham Road. There he worked at his little furnace with his apprentices wearing fire-resisting aprons. We came to know Mrs Ramsden, a quiet homely soul and most sympathetic, and I actually handled the fabulous gold and jewelled badge and chain which Ramsden made for the Worshipful Company of Master Mariners. In those days he must have been in his sixties, going grey with dark eyes and great patience.

The reminiscences raise a few thoughts; did Ramsden have a small workshop adjoining St Dunstan's and did he have men working there? I have come across no other reference to such a place. The description of his wife Anne as a quiet, homely soul is at odds with all other opinions of her, including that of her daughter and three grandchildren, but no doubt she would be helpful and polite to customers. The jewel and collar was made in 1929–30, perhaps Ramsden had borrowed it in the mid-thirties for display in an exhibition, as he did sometimes.

In February 1986 Phillips placed an advertisement in *The Times* to attract customers who might be considering selling silver in their sales. Two goblets by Ramsden, part of a set of six, were illustrated to catch their readers' attention, one with a thistle, the other with holly. They had realised £3,800 in a previous sale.

January 1987 brought a report by their saleroom correspondent Geraldine Norman on a silver sale at Christie's of twentieth century British works of art. She reported that 'Prices ran sharply ahead of expectations'. Ramsden's bowl of 1931 in 'pseudo- Medieval spirit' sold for £4,400 (estimate £1,200–£1,500) to Hancock and Co., the London dealers. It was the *Fauns and Dryads Bowl* originally commissioned by Waldo S. Skinner. Other Ramsden and Carr pieces also sold well above their estimates.

On 2 February 1988, the Royal Scottish Museum (now part of National Museums Scotland) added a 1910/11 presentation cup by Ramsden and Carr to their collection, bought from A. D. C. Heritage in a fair at the Dorchester Hotel. Though probably not shown since its acquisition, it is hoped that it will become part of the new gallery *Design For Living*, opened in Edinburgh in 2016.[7]

In December 1988, Conal Gregory advised in *The Times, Family Money*, that antiques were a beautiful and good investment. At that period furniture was the best investment, especially quality Edwardian and Victorian pieces. Arts and Crafts furniture makers such as Peter Waals, Ernest Gimson and Gordon Russell were recommended and are still desirable thirty years later. For antique silver he named George Fox and Omar Ramsden for work that should appreciate.

In April 2001 Clare Stewart wrote about collecting decorative work of the Arts and Crafts period. One of the highest estimates in a sale at Christie's had been for a Ramsden silver and moonstone box with an enamelled galleon on the lid. Estimated to raise £10,000, reflecting its high quality, it was illustrated in the paper. Always a popular Arts and Crafts motif, a galleon painted on six tiles by William de Morgan was shown on the same page. De Morgan had a pottery in Sands End, Fulham, until 1907, close to Ramsden and Carr's Maxwell Road workshop. Their time in Fulham would have overlapped by about four years, though whether they were acquainted is not known. We know that Ramsden and Carr admired his work as the 1914 photographs of the dining room at St Dunstan's show a dresser holding several plates on the top shelf which are almost certainly by de Morgan, decorated with his typical stylised fish.

In April 2004 John Russell Taylor reviewed *Silver and the Church, Treasures from London Churches*, an exhibition in the Goldsmiths' Hall. Under the title, Blessed Release, he stated that:

> Omar Ramsden's designs from the 1920s and 1930s also remind us that there was a major revival in artistic silversmithing at the time.

Ramsden's ecclesiastical commissions must have run into the hundreds, those in larger churches, abbeys or cathedrals can often be admired in the security of their treasuries, but viewing the many sacred vessels belonging to smaller churches can be very difficult because of security problems. Russell Taylor advised that 'the only reasonably secure means of public access is to lend the objects to a museum'. NADFAS – The National Association of Decorative and Fine Art Societies is compiling lists of such objects of interest in individual churches but has to exercise discretion regarding silver with a high financial value.

The interest and admiration for the work of both Ramsden and Carr obviously continues. What conclusions can we draw? Carr's work is highly collectible, though less widely identified. Much of it must be out of the public eye, in private hands. There is no evidence of Carr giving any lectures, he seems to have been much less self-assured and confident about public speaking and preferred to live quietly. Unlike Gerald Downs Butcher/Berriffe who attempted to disguise his homosexuality through three failed marriages, Alwyn Carr developed an enduring relationship with Arthur Hughes, carefully managing to live discreetly and avoid focus on his private life. In this he showed great courage and truth to himself. The evidence of the works he made has to be sufficient to show his skill and originality, they certainly provided him with financial success.

Ramsden was a much more confident and outgoing character, full of enthusiasm for his work, his family and for other people. Reading accounts of his lectures and articles has proved the best way to clarify what he actually said and thought, rather than relying on opinions attributed to him by other people.

Even as recently as July 2014 Father John Hunwicke exhorted readers of his blog to:

> Go to Westminster, a reminder that there is a delightful little permanent exhibition in Westminster Cathedral, well worth its entrance fee… What strikes you as you enter is a massive and gorgeous monstrance by Omar Ramsden, [unhappily no mention of Alwyn Carr] a characteristic product in Art Nouveau/Arts and Crafts. Go and wonder at it.

At the beginning of this search, I had no idea what I might find. When I first began to read the articles I could find about Ramsden and to talk to other people, I began to hear criticism of the man and his work which was often couched in exactly the same phrases, suggesting a single source; claiming that he had little skill himself in designing, drawing or making. At the same time I found that in spite of this there have continuously been many ardent enthusiasts for his work which has always been valued and sought after. My searches led me to the conclusions I have detailed in the text, that the only known account of his life was to be found in the notorious 1973 catalogue and that this unsupported view was neither impartial nor objective. I have tried to present a more balanced view, through examining contemporary critiques of his work in the journals of the most prestigious Arts and Crafts institutions of his day, and the record of his own words and opinions. The look into his early and later family life, and the memories of his wife's descendants, give a picture of a man I would like to have known, a warm and sociable family man as well as an outstanding craftsman.

1 *Goldsmiths' Journal,* January 1941, vol.43, *Omar Ramsden's Works For Sheffield.*

2 *Antiques Trade Gazette, Ramsden's Loving Spoonful,* 15 December 2001, no.1518.

3 *The Times,* 17 October 1947, p1.

4 ibid 10 November 1949.

5 ibid 2 July 1951, p8.

6 Catalogue, Spink Auction House, *60 Years of English Silver,* 1984.

7 Correspondence from Dr Sally Ann Huxtable, Principal Curator of Modern and Contemporary Design, 6 October 2015.

Acknowledgements

With many thanks to my generous sponsors:

The present owner of St. Dunstan's Studio

Rhoddy Voremberg

Alastair Dickenson

Especial thanks also to Ralph Holt, John, Maria and the late Paul Hallam, Simon Gilmore and Walt Ibbotson.

So many others have been very generous with their interest and research, in no particular order they include Clare Starkie, Curator of Decorative Art at Museums Sheffield, who was encouraging right at the start, John Kelly, Anne Wells, Anne and John Shannon, Hugh Whitehouse, Vicki Priestly, Walt Ibbotson, Robert Omar Ibbotson, David Beasley, Con Mercer, Judy Payne, Ian Pickford, Margaret Willins, Eliza Buckingham, Will Griffiths, James Hawkes, Tom Hughes and the late Betty Hughes, Jan Parkinson and David Baldwin of the Abbotsbrook Residents Association, Bourne End, Mike Butcher, David Burton, Alison Hodgkinson, Anthony Lester, Patrick Baty of the 21st Special Air Service Regiment (Artists) (Reserve), Eric Turner, Keeper of Metalwork Collections at the V&A, Gilly King of Whitelands College, Jeffrey Lassaline of Christies, Stephen Burton of Hancocks, Carole and Jan Van den Bosch, Lieutenant Colonel Richard C. Cole-Mackintosh, Clerk to the Worshipful Company of Shipwrights, Alison Harris at the Worshipful Company of Master Mariners. Last, but by no means least, my editor Lucie Skilton, who has provided so many creative suggestions, as have family and friends, to whom the name of Omar Ramsden has become so familiar.